best sex writing
2009

best sex writing 2009

Edited by
Rachel Kramer Bussel

CLEIS
PRESS

Published in the United States by
Cleis Press Inc., P.O. Box 14697, San Francisco, California 94114.

Printed in the United States.
Cover design: Scott Idleman
Cover photograph: Christine Kessler
Text design: Frank Wiedemann
Logo art: Juana Alicia
First Edition.
10 9 8 7 6 5 4 3 2 1

"One Rape, Please (to Go)" by Tracie Egan was originally published in *Vice* magazine, Vol.14 No.8. "Searching for Normal" by Lynn Harris was originally published on Nerve.com, February 26, 2008. "Father Knows Best" by Amanda Robb was originally published in *Marie Claire*, July 2007. "An Open Letter to the Bush Administration" by Mistress Morgana Maye was originally published in *Sex for America: Politically Inspired Erotica* (Harper Perennial) edited by Stephen Elliott, 2008. "The Pleasure of Unpleasure" by Kristina Lloyd was originally published on Lust Bites (lustbites.blogspot.com), October 1, 2007. "What's 'Normal' Sex?" by Brian Alexander was originally published on MSNBC.com, May 22, 2008. "Unleash the Beast" by "Josephine Thomas" was originally published in *Over the Hill and Between the Sheets: Sex, Love, and Lust in Middle Age* (Springboard Press) edited by Gail Belsky, 2008. "Is Cybersex Cheating?" by Violet Blue was originally published on SFGate.com, July 17, 2008. "Sex Offenders!!" by Kelly Davis was originally published in *San Diego City Beat*, April 15, 2008. "War Games" by Tom Johansmeyer was originally published in AVN Online, November 2007. "In Defense of Casual Sex" by Tracy Clark-Flory: this article first appeared in Salon.com, August 1, 2008. An online version remains in the Salon archives. Reprinted with permission. "Soulgasm" by Dagmar Herzog was originally published in *Sex in Crisis: The New Sexual Revolution and the Future of American Politics* (Basic Books) by Dagmar Herzog, 2008. Reprinted by permission of Basic Books , a member of Perseus Books Group. "Sexual Problems…" by Don Vaughan was originally published in *Penthouse Forum*, November 2007. "Penises I Have Known" by Daphne Merkin was originally published in *Playboy*, June 2007. "Sex Is the Most Stressful Thing in the Universe" by Dan Vebber was originally published in *Things I've Learned from Women Who've Dumped Me* (Grand Central Publishing) edited by Ben Karlin, 2008. "Silver-Balling" by Stacey D'Erasmo was originally published in *Dirty Words: A Literary Encyclopedia of Sex* (Bloomsbury) edited by Ellen Sussman, 2008. "Sex Dolls for the Twenty-First Century" by David Levy was originally published in *Love and Sex with Robots: The Evolution of Human-Robot Relationships* (Harper) by David Levy, 2007. "Dear John" by Susannah Breslin was originally published on Newsweek.com, May 26, 2008. "Oldest Profession 2.0" by Keegan Hamilton was originally published in *River Front Times*, June 4, 2008. "How 'Swingers' Might Save Hollywood from a Federal Pornography Statute" by Alan Levy was originally published in *Yale Law Journal Pocket Part*, April 28, 2008. "Why Bathroom Sex Is Hot" by James Hannaham: this article first appeared in Salon.com, August 31, 2007. An online version remains in the Salon archives. Reprinted with permission. "Kids and Comstockery, Back (and Forward) in the Day" by Debbie Nathan was originally published on Debbienathan.com, June 1, 2008. "The Immaculate Orgasm" by Mary Roach was originally published in *Bonk: The Curious Coupling of Science and Sex* (W.W. Norton) by Mary Roach, 2008.

CONTENTS

vii Foreword • Brian Alexander

x Introduction: Sex Is Everywhere • Rachel Kramer Bussel

1 One Rape, Please (to Go) • Tracie Egan

9 Searching for Normal: Do Dating Websites for People with STIs Liberate or Quarantine? • Lynn Harris

17 Father Knows Best • Amanda Robb

27 An Open Letter to the Bush Administration • Mistress Morgana Maye

31 The Pleasure of Unpleasure • Kristina Lloyd

36 What's "Normal" Sex? • Brian Alexander

43 Unleash the Beast • "Josephine Thomas"

52 Is Cybersex Cheating? • Violet Blue

57 Sex Offenders!! • Kelly Davis

69 War Games: No WMDs but Military Police Find "Dangerous" Dildos in Iraq • Tom Johansmeyer

77 In Defense of Casual Sex • Tracy Clark-Flory

85 Soulgasm • Dagmar Herzog

98 Sexual Problems: A Common Side Effect of Combat-Related PTSD • Don Vaughan

108 Penises I Have Known • Daphne Merkin

121 Sex Is the Most Stressful Thing in the Universe • Dan Vebber

129 Silver-Balling • Stacey D'Erasmo

132   Sex Dolls for the Twenty-First Century • David Levy

144   Dear John • Susannah Breslin

148   Oldest Profession 2.0: A New Generation of Local "Providers" and "Hobbyists" Create a Virtual Red-Light District • Keegan Hamilton

163   How "Swingers" Might Save Hollywood from a Federal Pornography Statute • Alan Levy

171   Why Bathroom Sex Is Hot • James Hannaham

176   Kids and Comstockery, Back (and Forward) in the Day • Debbie Nathan

182   The Immaculate Orgasm: Who Needs Genitals? • Mary Roach

197   About the Authors

204   About the Editor

Foreword

Brian Alexander

"Sex writing" is a loaded term. Any term with "sex" as one of its parts is loaded, I suppose, but "sex writing" has a certain cachet among writers and publishers, and it's not a good one. While "sex" may sell, sex writing has the reputation of being not only lowbrow, but lousy.

The term evokes images of cliché-ridden scenes, all sweat and moaning and inane talk. Ironic prizes are given for that sort of thing. Even great writers stumble over intercourse, oral sex, kink. How many naughty words are too many? Which euphemisms work and which ones sound uncomfortably junior high? How much detail is just too much? The possible double entendres alone are enough to frustrate basic composition. In the paragraph that follows this one, I wanted to use the phrase—grappling with sex—then thought better of it because I pictured something altogether too Greco-Roman.

In these pages you are not only going to find a variety of answers to these style questions, but, more importantly, a variety of answers to the larger question of how Americans are adapting (the grappling was going to go here) to new opportunities for sexual exploration. You may sharply disagree with the views of some writers, agree with others, and utter more than one "Eww!" as you read, but you if you pay attention, you will find a remarkable portrait of the great Technicolor rainbow mash-up of American sex.

We live in a country in which, contrary to our reputation, there are almost no rules adults are expected to obey when it comes to sex (though there are many rules some people wish we would all obey). How are we making sense of the new online sex world? Is such a thing even possible? Sex dolls? (I mean, really, sex dolls?) What's going on at the intersection of feminism and sexuality? Some sort of redefinition, sure, but "One Rape, Please (to Go)" by Tracie Egan? Daphne Merkin, in "Penises I Have Known," braves peer pressure to fess up that she likes men, or at least one part of them, and isn't it about time a woman said so?

Of course every revolution leaves some people behind, and trying to keep up with that group of people I call "sexual hipsters" can be a little unnerving. In his hilarious "Sex Is the Most Stressful Thing in the Universe," Dan Vebber says what many men wish we could say even if we haven't had his astounding bad luck. And, as the writer of a sex column for MSNBC.com and author of a book about American sex, I have personally experienced the dread of being caught out as hopelessly clueless that Stacey D'Erasmo encounters in "Silver-Balling."

How do we regulate this explosion of sex? Should we try? Who gets to do what to whom and how? Sex crime is a real problem, of course, but how do we handle sex offenders? Kelly Davis raises provocative questions that run counter to the conventional wisdom. Should a soldier be able to have a dildo in a combat zone? Is prostitution really a victimless crime? America's incessant push-pull over sex often takes place in courtrooms and police dockets and here you'll find some interesting examinations of the weird legal quilt we have woven.

Rachel Kramer Bussel, the primary editor most responsible for this collection, has done a bang-up job (see what I mean?) of selecting representative examples of America's changing sex life. Think of it as an album of snapshots from which you can get a good idea of your neighbor's summer vacation, without having to sit for all those hours in a hot car driving past the Bob's Big Boys and the sketchy fireworks stands before you get to the good parts.

Introduction: Sex Is Everywhere

Sex is everywhere—in our bedrooms, classrooms, courtrooms, and offices, as well as on our TV and movie screens, streets, and newspapers. This was a big year for sex, from prostitution (Eliot Spitzer, Ashley Dupré, Deborah Jeane Palfrey) to teen pregnancy (Jamie Lynn Spears, Bristol Palin) and beyond.

You don't have to look far to find sex, but you do have to get a bit bolder when looking for writing and thinking about sex that doesn't play to the lowest common denominator. The essays and articles here explore the big, bad (and good) world of sex in many forms, from online personals sites (for those with STIs) to impassioned arguments for casual sex (and bathroom sex—sometimes one and the same, sometimes not), as well as affairs, purity balls, penises, cybersex, and more.

As I said earlier, sex is everywhere—including on the battlefields of Iraq. We may think of sex and war as mutually exclusive terrains, but as Don Vaughan's story about sexual dysfunction and combat-related PTSD and Tom Johansmeyer's "War Games,"—which looks at one contractor's and two female soldiers' penalization for possessing porn and dildos, respectively—make clear, the two are intricately linked. In fact, there's no area of our lives where sex doesn't play a role, even (or perhaps, especially) religion. In "Soulgasm," an excerpt from Dagmar Herzog's excellent book *Sex in Crisis: The New Sexual Revolution and the Future of American Politics,* she looks at what Christian sex educators are saying about sex (from oral to anal to vibrators), and their advice may very well surprise you.

Our current mores and rules about sex didn't spring up out of nowhere, as Debbie Nathan shows in her exploration of early twentieth-century vice czar Anthony Comstock.

The personal stories here are ones I think may best illuminate how complex, individualistic, confusing, and profound sex can be. In "One Rape, Please (to Go)," Tracie Egan boldly starts out, "I blame my recurring rape fantasy on the fact that I'm a feminist." If that's not enough to keep you reading, I'll give you a clue as to what happens next: she hires a man to pretend to rape her, but what she gets in return is not quite what she bargained for. Similarly, in Dan Vebber's "Sex Is the Most Stressful Thing in the Universe," the goal of finally having sex becomes exalted to the point of mania, with a little help from his overly neurotic girlfriend.

I'd like to give special thanks to Miriam Axel-Lute and the Sex Positive Journalism Awards (aka the Sexies). This project was launched in order "to recognize the times when journalists stick to the standards of their craft in the face of such challenges and produce good, informative journalism that spreads accurate sexual information, stays fair in covering highly charged topics, and celebrates healthy sexuality as a positive force in people's lives." "War Games" by Tom Johansmeyer, was one of their runners–up for Sex-

Themed Publications, and all of their winners are worth reading (see sexies.org).

There were many extraordinary pieces I was not able to include in this book. Please visit bestsexwriting2009.wordpress.com for links to some of these pieces and to read more about the latest in sex.

With *Best Sex Writing 2008,* many people said they'd expected something far juicer from the racy cover. If you're looking for the latest jerk-off material, please check Cleis Press's website (www.cleispress.com) for their many fine erotica offerings; this is not one of those books, though some of these stories may titillate you or spark your erotic imagination. I always recall that the brain is the biggest sex organ. Learning about sex can inspire us to be better, more knowledgeable, and more empathetic lovers, family members, and citizens.

I hope this book will open your mind and make you think about your own sexuality, as well as your neighbors', politicians', and best friends'. It's given me plenty of food for thought, and I'm grateful that sex continues to challenge us to think, explore, and appreciate its many nuances.

Rachel Kramer Bussel

One Rape, Please (to Go)
Tracie Egan

I blame my recurring rape fantasy on the fact that I'm a feminist. I've never made any bones about getting boned in exactly the fashion that I want. But as a girl, my equipment can be trickier to manage, therefore I need to be a boss in the bedroom to ensure I get worked the right way. It gets really tiresome always being the one in charge, and don't shrinks say that people usually fantasize about the opposite of their reality? I guess that's why I find myself wishing that my typically sugary-sweet sexual encounters were sometimes peppered with assault. I decided that the best way to forfeit that control—while still holding on to a modicum of it for safekeeping—would be to hire someone for the job. Not to put too fine a point on it, I wanted a male whore to rape me.

My first thoughts were of New York artist Brock Enright, who founded Video Games Adventure Services in 2002. It's a company that provides a rather violent "designer kidnapping" for a price that actually rapes a wallet more than it does the customer, but I'd heard tell that some escort services provide similarly realistic rape and abduction scenarios for a fraction of the cost. I didn't want mine to be crazy violent, with, like, punching and stuff. (I wouldn't mind some fingerprint bruises on my wrists, but my face needs to stay pretty so I can keep getting sex for free on other occasions.) I also didn't want any duct tape involved, and I didn't want to be gagged (unless, you know, it's with a cock).

And so began my quest to hire a rapist. I started by reviewing hustlers' profiles through escort websites, but I was totally turned off. Even when they said they only serviced women, they all looked like total homos. Don't get me wrong, I have nothing against gay dudes. I just don't want to get raped by one. I knew they wouldn't be "up" for the job, har har har. I actually had a lot more luck in the "erotic services" section of Craigslist. I didn't have to go through a middleman, and all the dudes I corresponded with were more than happy to send me cock shots, free of charge.

The pictures were really important to me. One of my main concerns about hiring a hooker was that he might be ugly. I'm not one of those girls that needs an emotional connection to fuck a guy. Shit, I don't even need to know his last name. But he needs to be attractive. Swagger and wit can only get one so far. I'm into faces. And I wasn't sure I could get into it if he had an ugly one. I decided he would need to wear a ski mask, because then I wouldn't know if he was ugly, and because it would also be extra scary and thrilling and hot. Of the dudes on my short list, only one of them had a ski mask. But he also mentioned in the same sentence that he had a gun we could use, and thus ended his brief tenure on my short list.

I ended up making a date with a twenty-one-year-old guy (let's call him Dick) who said that he exclusively services women. I liked him because in the picture he sent to my phone, he wasn't ugly. He looked half-Guido, half-frat-boy, and that seemed like a pretty rape-y combo. He assured me he could handle the rape fantasy, as role-playing was his specialty. Dick said he would perform the whole fantasy, with no time limit, for three hundred dollars.

Even though he wasn't heinous looking, I still wanted him to wear a ski mask. Because of my preconceived notions about hookers regarding their reliability and character in general, I decided that I'd take the reins on procuring the mask. I made the trek to a large sporting-goods store only to find out that ski masks weren't in season. Oh, well. As I left the store, sans ski mask, I was gripped with just how real this was. I was going to be face-to-face with my rapist in a few short hours. I called Dick up and told him that there was a change of plans. Instead of accosting me outside of my apartment building, we decided that the best way to go would be date rape. We agreed to meet at a bar in my neighborhood and get a few drinks first.

I went to the drugstore and picked up some condoms and some Tucks. I was so nervous that I was like borderline diarrhea. I knew he was just some whore, but I still didn't want to have a dirty butt in front of him. I also stopped at the liquor store, bought two bottles of wine, and began drinking as soon as I got home, to help me relax.

About an hour before our date, I got a text from Dick: "Yo, I don't want to charge for this."

I texted back, "If it's all the same, I'd rather just keep the arrangement as we have it." He responded with, "Are you a cop?"

Oh, God, I thought. I called Dick up and explained to him that I didn't want to get raped for free, because I felt that the exchange of money was the only way I'd be able to maintain the small amount of power I needed to feel comfortable. Besides, at this point, a large part of the allure of this whole thing was that I was actually going to fuck a hooker. Giving me a freebie would've robbed me of that opportunity. I set him straight and an hour later, I got a text letting me know he was at the bar. It said: "I'm here babe."

As I walked up the street toward the bar, I could see him having a smoke outside. He was cute enough, but skinnier than his picture, and he looked younger than twenty-one. I'm twenty-eight. *Christy,* I thought, *who's raping who here?*

We hugged briefly, then went inside and began pounding vodka sodas to cut the tension. I was pleasantly surprised that Dick immediately took control. He decided that our safeword would be "surprise," and he told me that he was just going to keep coming on as strong as possible, until he heard me say the word. We played a few rounds of Erotic Photo Hunt on the bar's Megatouch. I was taking the game sort of seriously, but he wasn't really paying attention to it. He kept pushing his face into my neck, and saying stupid yet appropriate things, like, "Oh, you're such a dirty girl," and, "Yeah, I like when you touched her titty," referring to the naked girl in the game. He put on the full-court press, groping my boobs and reaching his hand down between my legs, beneath my minidress.

By this point, I was sufficiently drunk and getting turned on by his dirtbag display. My tights were soaking wet (which he, of course, pointed out). I began to think I wasn't really cut out to play the victim, because I was fighting my inner slut, which ached to push my crotch toward his hand, instead of pulling away like my fantasy required. I knew it was time to get the show on the road, before I ended up ruining the whole thing by dragging him into the bar bathroom to fuck him in one of the stalls.

We got back to my building and climbed the four floors to my apartment, with him trailing behind, goosing me the whole way. As soon as we got inside, he started in with a DFK (that's hooker for "deep French kiss") on my couch.

"Let's go to your room," he breathed in my ear. I was about to be like, "Fuck, yeah," but then I remembered why we were here, so instead I said, "Oh, I don't know."

"Yeah, come on," he insisted, as he got up from the couch and pulled me toward my bedroom.

We sat on the bed and he started kissing me again. He pushed me down and I tried to politely nudge him away and sit back up, but he wouldn't let me. *Whoa,* I thought, *this is really happening! Holy fucking shit!* He grabbed my wrists and held them down with one hand as he started frantically undoing his pants with the other. I tried to wriggle free, but I was pinned.

"Don't act like you don't fucking want it, you little bitch," he sneered.

That's actually when I began really fighting him, because I wanted to be sure that he put a condom on before anything else happened. The last thing I need in my life is a trick baby. Or HPV. I reached toward my nightstand and grabbed the strip of condoms I'd carefully laid out earlier in the evening.

He lifted my dress up over my head, so I couldn't see what he was doing, and we began a tug of war with my tights, with me trying to keep them on, and him trying to rip them off. The struggle went on for maybe ninety seconds before my tights gave way. He jammed it in.

One Mississippi, two Mississippi, and he came. Literally, two fucking seconds, and it was over. *Hmm,* I thought, *I wonder if this is what it's like with real rape.* It makes sense. Rapists are probably not too worried about premature ejaculation. It behooves them to get it over with fast.

Dick immediately began apologizing, saying, "It's just that you're so sexy. Give me a minute. I'll get hard again. Let me just collect myself." But I drowned out the sound of his voice with the sound of my vibrator. There was no fucking way I wasn't coming after all of that. He tried to make amends by putting his fingers in me, but I swatted his hand away, saying only, "Surprise."

Within a few minutes I came twice, then tossed the vibe on the floor. Dick just stared at me the whole time. Again, he tried touching my pussy, now tender from having been properly massaged. "Surprise!" I hissed it this time, before shooting up off my bed and stumbling into my living room.

I poured myself a glass of wine, plopped down on my couch, grabbed the remote, and scanned the TV. Dick emerged from my room, wearing only his boxers. He sat down next to me and rubbed my thigh. "I want to make you come again," he whispered in my ear. I laughed in his face.

"You're so cute, how you always giggle at what I say," and then he started in with another DFK. This time, when I closed my eyes, my head began spinning and I realized just how drunk I was. I thought I might puke in his mouth, so I pushed him away.

"Why don't you get your clothes on," I said.

"No, I want to go one more time. C'mon. You know you want it."

He wouldn't let it up. So finally I was forced to yet again yell out, "Surprise! Get dressed. It's time for you to leave."

He got his clothes on and as he was tying his shoes, I reached into my bag and pulled out an envelope filled with the cash he was owed, plus an extra fifty dollars as a tip. I handed it to him, and he said, "I still feel bad that it ended so quickly."

"Yeah," I said. "You're right." So I reached in the envelope and removed two of the twenties. "This is for the drinks I bought." I thought for a minute, reached back in, and grabbed another, saying,

"And this is for coming too fast." I put his sixty-dollar docked pay in my wallet.

He hung his head and said, "Yeah, that's only fair."

I called him a cab and literally had to push him out of my place. He kept trying to hug me and gently kiss me all over my face. I grimaced as I ducked and dodged his attempts at intimacy or cuddling, or whatever the hell he was trying to do. As soon as he was gone, I sunk back into my couch. About five minutes later I received a text from him: "You sure? I just wanna make u come again and that's it."

Ugh! What the hell made him think he did it the first time? I ignored him. Six minutes later I received another text: "Oh great. Story of my life ha ha. I'll talk with you soon I hope."

I ignored that one as well. Eight minutes later I received another text: "But hey seriously you were amazing. Def give me a call some time soon."

I hadn't answered the first two, so I didn't bother answering this one either. I drank my wine and eventually passed out on my couch. My phone woke me up several hours later, at around one A.M. It was him! I pressed ignore with more purpose than I ever have in my life. I saw that there were two new text messages as well. One was at 11:54 P.M., about two and a half hours after Dick left my place. It said, "You still up? I bet u are...call me."

The other message was a picture that Dick took of himself—naked and wearing only a bow tie. The text said, "I really like you."

Oh, my God. I ordered a rape and was served a stalker. A little after three A.M. I received one last text for the night, "You still awake? I miss u."

In the morning, I checked my email, and what do you know? It's Dick in my box! He wrote, "Hey little lady, sorry for calling you so much last night. I guess I was a lot drunker than I thought.

LOL! But really, you are great, and I'd love to see you again. We should really hang out again."

I wrote him back, saying only, "Yeah, I was really drunk, too. Take care." That seemed like a sufficient kiss-off to me.

Two days later, guess who called me? Hi, Mr. Clingy Prostitute. I never took any of his calls ever again, nor returned his texts or emails.

You know what really pisses me off? People are always quick to accuse girls of too easily becoming emotionally attached after they sleep with a guy. But I've never heard of any call girl who tried to hang out with a John for free because she liked him so much. It just wouldn't happen. Women are far more capable of compartmentalizing issues of love and sex and work and play than people (dudes) give us credit for.

So, considering the way we each handled ourselves after our business transaction, it turns out that I'm the dick—and he's a pussy.

Searching for Normal: Do Dating Websites for People with STIs Liberate or Quarantine?
Lynn Harris

Kurt, a twenty-four-year-old Arizona man with HPV, lives in the kind of community where everybody knows everybody—a fact that makes dating with a sexually transmitted infection difficult. "Women have been interested in me, but I've just blown them off, even when I've been extremely interested," he says. "These women are always within my circles, and the possibility of people close to me finding out scares me to no end."

So he turned to dating websites that cater specifically to people with STIs. "It gets the monkey off your back right away," he says. "I can feel comfortable getting to know someone and not be thinking, *How am I going to tell her?*"

Problem is, Kurt hasn't experienced this liberation. He hasn't met anyone he likes through these services, and hasn't had sex—or even a date—in several years.

Dating websites for people with the same STI seem like a natural niche, one that includes PositiveSingles.com, H-Date.com, and the genre's warhorse, MPwH.com (Meet People with Herpes), which was founded in 1997 and has more than 70,000 active members. Newcomer PositiveFriends.com has a photo-editing application that allows you to upload photos that obscure your identity, zooming in on just your tattoo or your eyes. Another new site, VDdate.com, feels a bit rickety with its use of outdated terminology like "venereal disease," but its presence reinforces the point: many STI sufferers are opting out of the general singles population and sticking to their own private dating pool.

Or ghetto, depending on who you're talking to. "Creating specific Internet-dating sites for persons with STDs tends to perpetuate stigma by separating them from the general population," says Jeffrey D. Klausner, MD, director of STD Prevention and Control Services at the San Francisco Department of Public Health. "This isolation suggests that those persons are different and not normal, requiring exceptional means to meet other partners."

"Your self-worth is taken the minute you sign up for one of those sites. You're reduced to believing that you're confined to finding a mate afflicted with the same STI as you," says John Jackson, who cofounded the social-networking site Club462.com as an alternative to the dating-by-niche approach; it is openly inclusive of people with STIs. "The reality is that most people will accept you the way you are, once they know you," he adds, citing three cases of negative-positive romance sparked on his site.

This is not always the case. Jackson recalls showing his brother an STI-dating site as an example of what he didn't want to create. His brother's response: "I guess infected skanks need a place to go, too."

We're supposedly living in an era of sexual enlightenment—BDSM has become pedestrian, furries garner yawns. Yet many people with sexually transmitted infections still feel like members of a second-class citizenry. Blame it on our obsession with health and cleanliness: for many people, a significant other with herpes doesn't mesh with the ideal yoga-and-pomegranate lifestyle. Unlike most other illnesses, STIs are regarded as distasteful, even disgraceful.

This; even though STIs are more common than ever. Calling their spread a "hidden epidemic," the CDC estimates there are 18.9 million new infections each year. At least half of the sexually active population will contract HPV at some point; 80 percent of women will have it by age fifty. Herpes Simplex Virus (HSV) is at 1.6 million new cases a year: one in five adults, whether they know it or not, has herpes right now. After a precipitous drop, HIV diagnoses have been climbing slightly since 2001. It's estimated that nearly half a million Americans are living with HIV or AIDS.

And these are just the people who know what they've got—viral STIs are sometimes asymptomatic and frequently go undiagnosed. Statistically, your date is more likely to carry a sexually transmitted infection than to share your astrological sign.

You'd think the sheer magnitude of the epidemic would serve to defuse the associated shame, but the stigma surrounding STIs remains virulent and pervasive. They are, after all, about sex—stereotypically, about casual, unprotected sex. They're also, stereotypically, about hideous sores that bloom where the sun doesn't shine. In a survey conducted for Novartis Pharmaceuticals, a majority of respondents said they wouldn't date someone with herpes, and more than a quarter said herpes held more stigma than HIV.

"If someone I met online told me they had an STD, I'd be like, 'Yuck,'" says Katie, thirty-seven, of Austin, Texas. "And I have herpes."

So it's not hard to see why, for many people, STI-dating sites are a godsend. "You already know that that person has herpes, so [there's] no fretting over when to bring it up," says Betsy O'Rourke, thirty-nine, a pediatric nurse and herpes-patient advocate who is herself a herpes carrier and user of both STI and mainstream dating sites. "There's no wondering if it's going to be a deal-breaker for them. You can relax about that part and focus instead on finding out what's wrong with them," she laughs. That big reveal is a big, big issue, judging from the message-board topics at H-Date.com: "When should I tell?"; "Will they flip and run away?"; "What are your chances with a non-herpster?"

Those community features can inject a sense of normalcy into the dating process. "There are people there who understand," says Jodi Matthews, owner of Antopia, the parent company of MPwH. com and its sister sites. "You see normal, everyday people. They have herpes, and they're having fun. You realize, 'My diagnosis is manageable. I can have fun, I can have a meaningful, productive, loving life.' It's a place where herpes is not an issue anymore. It's home."

But do these dating services imply, as Dr. Klausner believes, that people with STIs should date only amongst themselves? Or at least, that they're destined to be seen as attractive only to other people with an illness?

"We talked about this long before we launched," says Michael Hummel, founder of PositiveFriends.com. "We decided that it's very similar to JDate. Is JDate relegating Jews to only date other Jews? No. It's a place where people have something in common and are able to relate to each other."

Jodi Matthews, the owner of Antopia, uses a similar analogy: "If someone goes to a dating site for people with dogs, does that reinforce the thought that people with dogs should only date other people with dogs? No. It's just a common denominator."

But there's an obvious difference. HPV is not a hobby; JDate isn't thriving because of anti-Semitism. Jews and dog owners don't hesitate to put their photos on their profiles—or if they do, it's not because they observe Passover or own a puggle. "I have tried using almost every STD-dating site I could find, but with no success," says Kurt, that twentysomething from Tempe, Arizona with HPV. "I don't post a picture for fear of being recognized, though I know how foolish that is. If I posted a picture, I could probably get a date. But the fear stops me." In other words, most niche dating sites aren't seen as shelters from shame and persecution.

At least they're not in New York, where a Gentile dating a Jew is as controversial as an American professing a love of French culture. Hummel points out that in certain sections of the Heartland, JDate might be used similarly to the STI-dating sites—as a way to avoid an awkward conversation. "I would suggest that outside of the major U.S. cities there still exists a stigma for being Jewish. Even here in Michigan, I've had to explain what it means to be a Jew, and why I'm 'not wearing the funny little hat,'" he says. If we don't chastise Jews in small-minded communities for using JDate, why should we look down upon the notion of an isolated online dating world for STI sufferers?

Not everyone buys this argument. "I've heard many people say they think they're only 'allowed' to date within their STD. Many say that before they got infected, they wouldn't have thought of dating someone with an STD, so why would they expect someone else to date them now?" says thirty-nine-year-old A.J. from Portland, Maine, a moderator at the Original Herpes Home Page. "They're buying into the stigma, and I think STD-dating sites contribute to these feelings. When someone gets diagnosed with HSV, HPV, or another STD, they go home and start searching the Internet for information. One of the first things they see in the search results are all of the STD-dating sites. Right away, that can give the idea that a person with an STD is only supposed to date within that STD."

On a bad day, so can the community itself.

One reply to that H-Date query, "What are your chances with a non-herpster?" generated this blunt response: "THERE ARE NO CHANCES WITH A NON-HERPSTER." (For his part, A.J. thinks the chances are pretty good. "Having allergies affects my life more than herpes does. I have never been rejected because of herpes. One guy I told said, 'Okay, great. Now can we go get pizza?'")

There's also the danger that misconception can lead to additional infection. Epidemiologically speaking, just because you can skip The Talk doesn't necessarily mean you can toss the condoms. Two HPV-positive partners still need to talk about which of the numerous strains each of them carries; if they're not careful, one of them could wind up contracting something new. "Forgoing condoms because a couple is already infected with one STD will not protect from others," says Dr. Klausner of the San Francisco Department of Public Health. Fortunately, as common as herpes is, transmission is relatively rare under certain easily met conditions (antiviral meds, condoms, no sex during outbreaks).

But perhaps the most mundane danger of using STI dating sites exclusively is not meeting anyone at all—at least, no one near your zip code. "Some people will be rejected because of their STI—that's reality," says Terri Warren, a registered nurse and medical advisor for MPwH.com. "But you're really narrowing the pool when you're looking for someone who will both like your characteristics and tolerate your herpes. You can be mad at society for putting you in this 'inferior' category, but you have to be careful not to do the same thing to yourself."

To be fair, nowhere do these sites explicitly tell users that intra-STI dating is—or should be—their only option. Instead, they offer a "friendly place where a 'private issue' becomes a nonissue," says Matthews. "When someone walks into the chess club meeting in high school, they don't have to say, 'Hey, I'm interested in chess.' In the same way, MPwH sets up the common ground. Instead of providing a 'stigma-free zone,' we focus on showing people that they're not unusual or bad because they have a virus. Ninety percent of the discussion on our message boards is identical to what you'd see on a mainstream site—what do men think, what do women think, and other water-cooler conversations. People tell us all the time that herpes was the best thing that happened to them, because of the people they've met on MPwH."

For this reason, Terri Warren thinks STI dating services are ideal for newbies. "It can be very useful to put a profile in a place like MPwH.com when you're still pretty fragile," she says. "But the longer you have herpes, the less focused you are on that as the characteristic that defines you. And then maybe you begin to date a wider range of people. I see it as a great way to build up your nerve and then step back into the general population."

It's also worth debunking a final stereotype: not every STI sufferer is hunched miserably over a computer bemoaning his or her fate. For everyone with a string of rejection horror stories or a history of twice-shy celibacy, there's someone with a healthy dose of antiviral perspective (someone like the numerous people I interviewed for this article who shrugged and said "yes" when asked if I could identify them by their full names).

Or someone like Melanie, thirty-nine, of Nashville: "If every person felt like they had to choose a dating site based on their 'issue' or shortcoming, can you imagine how ridiculous the online dating world would be?" she says. "It's silly to think that people with low credit scores would be ushered to the 'bad-credit dating site,' or folks in recovery to the 'former-addict dating site.' "

Melanie uses mainstream dating sites, where, she notes, she's probably a much "safer" bet than people who say they're disease-free but don't get regular, comprehensive STI tests. "Bottom line: dating with an STD is not a big deal," she says. "At my age and with my life experience, herpes is nothing compared to relationship killers like debt, train-wreck ex-wives, infidelities, addictions, and man boobs."

Father Knows Best
Amanda Robb

Lauren Wilson Black, twenty-two, is the kind of kitten-faced, minx-bodied, all-American beauty who could break a dozen hearts with one bat of her silky lashes. But until last winter, Lauren had never seduced a boy into misery delicto—or even flirted. She'd never had a lover, made out in a guy's car, pressed against a boy during a slow dance at the high-school prom, or even been to a prom. Call her the anti-Lindsay/Paris/Britney. She was a super-virgin. While the rest of us spent our youthful years pushing the limits of what could be done in backseats and bar bathrooms, Lauren stayed home. Weird, you say?

Actually, not really. Six years ago, the National Longitudinal Study of Adolescent Health found that one in six Americans between the ages of twelve and eighteen had taken a purity pledge. That is, they vowed to remain virgins until marriage.

Among those virginity pledgers, courtship has become the

trend du jour. The brainchild of Josh Harris, a thirty-three-year-old Christian evangelical and author of *I Kissed Dating Goodbye,* courtship is the antihookup. No nooky. No commitment flake-outs. No playing the field. You see a stranger at the local mall or church barbecue, and then—if you both feel that certain spark—he asks your father if he can "court" you. Lauren's parents, Randy and Lisa, are on board, to say the least. In 1998, they founded the Father Daughter Purity Ball (think prom meets wedding reception). The formal event is attended by hundreds of teenage girls and their dads. After dinner and before dancing, the fathers sign an agreement—as the "high priests of the home"—to be their daughters' "authority and protector in the area of purity." In 2006, Purity Balls took place in forty-eight states; next April, the Wilsons will host New York City's first-ever Purity Ball at the Waldorf-Astoria.

I met the Wilsons while covering the Colorado Springs Father Daughter Purity Ball, which takes place at the city's five-star Broadmoor Hotel. To put it plainly, I was fully prepared for Randy, Lisa, and their children to be the biggest freaks I ever met. The concept of premarital virginity seemed archaic enough; the image of a father monitoring his daughter's sex life was fairly revolting. So I was nothing short of astonished to find the Wilsons likable.

It was through my conversations with Randy and Lisa about their Purity Balls that I developed a fascination with Lauren. Homeschooled since kindergarten and absent a college degree, Lauren experienced joys (feeling popular) and woes (being ostracized by friends whom she introduced!) that were nevertheless extraordinarily similar to those of my own—or, for that matter, most people's—adolescence. Still, when she was thirteen, Lauren decided to do something I could never fathom doing: give her heart to her dad so he could "save" it for her husband.

"I was just like, Why hang out with a guy, break your heart, hang out with the next guy, break your heart again?" Lauren says, when I ask her what she was thinking the day she told her dad she wanted to be a virgin until marriage. Randy is a sinewy man, who, in his khakis and polos, dresses the part of laid-back Westerner. But his grave blue eyes and careful, sonorous speech bespeak unstinting seriousness. The day of her announcement, he penned this letter:

> Dear Son-in-Law,
>
> By the time you sit down and read this, your wedding day will have passed...know we have had long talks about Lauren, but let me write them down...Lauren's heart is overflowing with love and care for others. She is unselfish almost to a fault. She waits for your leadership and will respond to you accordingly. Lauren has great inner strength and physical stamina, but she will need your God-given strength to function. She wants to please you like no other. Most importantly, Lauren needs your spiritual leadership. She needs you to take her to the throne of God...
>
> Love,
> Your Father-in-Law

For the next seven years, Lauren avoided boys altogether. Then, in February 2006, the Wilsons paid a visit to the Air Force Academy, which Lauren's brother Colten was considering attending. Accompanying the family on the tour was twenty-three-year-old Brett Black, a blond-haired cadet. Lauren had met him before through church, but "from that moment on," Lauren sighs, "I was just, like, head over heels."

She returned home that evening and asked God if Brett was the one for her. "I set aside forty days to really pray hard and ask for direction," she remembers. Meanwhile, Brett also decided that Lauren and her two teenage sisters were "gorgeous." The idea of a permanent commitment entered his mind.

"I thought, Am I crazy? I'm graduating in three months and possibly moving away," he says. "But I could see myself marrying one of those girls!" Brett, too, began to pray. The future pilot soon found himself being "guided toward Lauren." Two months later, he arranged to meet Randy at a coffee shop. There Brett said, "I'd like to start a relationship with one of your daughters." He thinks he specified Lauren. Randy invited him to dinner. After the meal, Lauren and Brett were left alone. "I've noticed your character and I'd like to hang out with you. I hope I don't sound stupid," he said. "It would be an honor," she said.

Over cappuccinos at the local Starbucks, Randy and Lisa share their theories about the success of Lauren's courtship. "I'm the one who knows Lauren," Randy explains, describing how he met with Brett every few weeks after their initial conversation for what amounted to marital coaching. "Brett doesn't know anything about Lauren. So I can help them be a success."

As much as I respect Randy's sincerity, I find his involvement in Lauren's relationship medieval. And if he doesn't appreciate that, surely Lisa—woman to woman—can see the peculiarity of this arrangement?

Lisa, a voluptuous, emotive blonde who will spend thirty-one years (1990 to 2021) homeschooling her seven children, sees no such thing. Her own father walked out on her family when she was two. "I felt like he threw my heart on the ground and said, 'Deal with it,'" says Lisa, bursting into tears. I pass her a napkin.

And Randy's father? "He was good at providing, poor at relationships," he says. Absent any examples, Randy and Lisa wrote their own rules.

After meeting at Ohio's Cedarville University, Randy and Lisa married in 1982. That year, they moved to Austin, Texas, where Randy started a roofing company. It dissolved in the mid-'80s, by which time the Wilsons had four small children. When Randy got a job offer in construction in Colorado, the family moved there, but soon after, the job evaporated.

"He pounded the pavement eight hours a day and couldn't get a job flipping burgers," says Lisa, who remained at home, caring for their children. After months of looking, Randy landed a position as a salesman for a print-media company—not exactly a financial coup.

In such difficult times, other men—and let's face it, women, too—might have taken to drinking, crime, or promiscuity. Some would have just taken off. Randy, however, took to the Lord.

After coffee with Randy and Lisa, I spend the evening trying to put Lauren's relationship into a context I can understand. I imagine my own husband receiving marital advice from members of my immediate family. ("Amanda can be bitchy, but if you bring her a bottle of chardonnay she cheers up considerably.") Depending on his mood, my husband would have burst out laughing or run screaming from my entire clan.

At a meeting with Brett in the spring of 2006, Randy raised the issue of displaying affection and how it can lead to sexual temptation. "From what I experience as a guy, the physical aspect of things just opens all kinds of doors for hormones," Randy told him. "Why open those doors now? It's a distraction from getting to know Lauren." Indeed. Lauren would later tell me that during their courtship—which included dinners alone, a skiing excursion, and a seven-day trip to Japan as part of a church missionary group—she and Brett never exchanged a kiss, or even so much as held hands.

Didn't she wonder what kissing and sex would be like? Lauren and I are spending a winter afternoon at the local salon getting pedicures (I want "Femme Fatale Red"; she wants something softer), and I can't help but use our time alone to press for more intimate details. "Of course," she says, "but it was just really hard to imagine, so I tried to focus on other things."

Did that work?

"Sometimes."

Did she masturbate?

Lauren suddenly looks like a Barbie doll—amiably expressionless. "I'm not going to answer that," she says.

"I wouldn't either," I say.

"Good," she says.

What she will say is that her courtship with Brett was emotionally hot. "We talked a lot," she says. "We asked each other intense questions like 'What's the saddest thing that's ever happened to you?' and 'What's the hardest thing you've been through?'"

Seven weeks into their relationship, Brett asked Randy if he could propose to Lauren. Randy said yes. Lauren and Brett are to become official partners on December 29, 2006, smack in the middle of a whiteout blizzard. I'm invited to the big event, and I'm determined to be there—despite it taking more than an hour to drive eight miles from my hotel to the Mountain Springs Church. Inside, the decor is simple: white candles, white-fabric columns framing the altar, a string quartet playing Bach. About two hundred and fifty people sit smiling; a serene pregnant woman next to me whispers that at least another one hundred can't make it due to the storm.

At exactly 5:10 P.M., seven trim, tuxedoed groomsmen enter and line up, perfectly spaced, followed by seven bridesmaids in black spaghetti-strapped sheaths, delicately picking their way up the aisle.

And finally, a radiant Lauren emerges in a tight-bodice, low-back, full-skirt gown (think Penélope Cruz in Atelier Versace at the 79th Academy Awards). Randy, who is officiating, takes his place at the altar. In his homily, he praises "the power and the beauty" of Lauren and Brett's choices. "To walk in purity in your relationship and engagement...has brought great honor to the throne of God and to your parents," he says. "Brett...I walked [you] through what Lauren's heart looked like. We talked of her incredible fragileness and the place that you must occupy for her to continue to grow into the fullness of all that God has created in her."

Everyone but me is smiling.

Soon enough, it's time for the inevitable. Randy seems to be stalling. "You know," he hems, "as soon as I do this next part, I lose all control." Finally, with tears standing in his eyes, he pronounces his daughter another man's wife. With that, Brett lifts Lauren's veil and kisses her. Lauren had told me she was afraid she'd faint when Brett's lips touched hers. I try to imagine what it would be like to experience my first-ever smooch in front of an audience of hundreds, but Lauren is fine. And her first kiss with Brett makes me teary, too—on the one hand because she looks so happy, on the other because she'll never know the sublime joy of kissing a beautiful-but-stupid jock, who, in your worst nightmare, you would never, ever marry.

"It awakened everything in me," Lauren says later of her first kiss. "It was beyond. I was just like, Wow!" "Wow" is also how she describes her first night with Brett after their wedding reception, when they checked in to the Broadmoor Hotel. An explicit promise of the virginity-until-marriage movement is that if you wait for the big day to have intercourse, the sex will be mind-blowing.

(A popular public-school sex-ed curriculum in Colorado is called "Wait Training: Learn How to Have the Best Sex—By Waiting Until Marriage!") In their hotel room, the first thing Lauren did was get a basin and water pitcher and wash Brett's feet.

Come again?

"My spiritual gift is serving," she explains. "And I wanted to show Brett, 'I'm here to love you, follow you, and serve you.'"

Oh.

After drying her new husband's feet, the night only got better. "It was incredible," Lauren says of losing her virginity.

I push for details.

She sticks to "incredible."

I describe the first time I had sex. I was seventeen, and my boyfriend's parents were out of town. My boyfriend (Bob), his buddy, my best friend (Jen), and I were at his house fooling around, and Jen came into Bob's bedroom and said, "I'll do it if you do it." We all did it. In Bob's bedroom there was some confusion about mechanics (hips synchronized or in opposition?), a bit of discomfort on my part, and a little performance anxiety on his. Afterward, Jen and I confabbed and decided that sex had "potential." Lauren nods and smiles.

I flat-out ask if she has orgasms. She defers with an "It's amazing."

Three weeks after their wedding, I visit Lauren at their apartment near Luke Air Force Base in Arizona, where Brett is temporarily stationed. She looks the same—smiling, doll-like. When we sit down to talk, Lauren tells me about a seventeen-year-old girl she met in the computer room of her new apartment complex. Crying, the girl told Lauren, "I think my fiancé's cheating on me, and I'm trying to figure out what to do because I'm pregnant with his kid."

"And I thought, Oh, that's really interesting," says Lauren. "She's had sex with him, and now she's opened the door to fear and rejection. What's she going to do if he leaves? She's got his child, she's only seventeen, she didn't graduate high school. Now what?"

Lauren thinks the trouble began when the couple had sex. I think the trouble began when that girl didn't use birth control. Before I've put these thoughts into words, Lauren continues. "For me," she says, "I'm stronger as a woman because I came into marriage as a virgin. I'm whole."

Despite my past lovers, I feel remarkably whole, too, and tell Lauren so.

"But when you've saved yourselves for only each other, there's trust," she says. "Now I'm able to give Brett everything. I know that I'm the only one who knows him intimately. I'm not afraid of, 'When is he going to ditch me?' or 'Will he cheat on me?'"

I hold the opposite view. It's kind of like dieting: limit me to vanilla wafers, and I'll be craving a bakery. And while I sampled many cookies before getting hitched, I never worry that either of us is going to stray.

That night in Arizona, Lauren, Brett, and I dine at a restaurant across from Wal-Mart called Mimi's. She wears a beaded gauzy top, he wears a T-shirt that shows off his admirable muscles. They sit side by side and share shy smiles, looking and acting like a couple who just met—which, in many ways, is what they are. Unlike my husband and me after we married, Lauren doesn't automatically know what Brett will order. He stares intently at Lauren when I ask her a question—not sure what she'll answer. He's amused to learn that Lauren feels like they are playing house; she's surprised that Brett feels guilty when he lingers at the base after work. They are great mysteries to each other, but even so—or maybe because of that—the sexual heat between them is palpable.

Lauren says she embraces her new life as a stay-at-home wife, spending her days cleaning, grocery shopping, decorating, emailing, "then waiting for Brett to get home." Though she misses her family, she's determined to succeed in her new role. "I see my life as helping Brett," she says. I tell her it sounds like she's giving up her personal freedom. She disagrees.

"Freedom," she says, "comes from living within boundaries. It's like driving. There are lanes and signs—which some might find constraining—but if they weren't there, it would be chaos." Stay in your lane, though, and it's easy to get where you want to go. Before I catch a plane back to New York, Lauren and I visit the mall to get our eyes done at a MAC cosmetics counter. Lauren looks modelesque in a range of plums; I look like a large leprechaun in a trio of lime greens. As we laugh together over that girly universal, eye shadow, you'd never know that Lauren fears for my marriage and maybe my soul, and I fear that she—a bright, passionate girl—is living a subjugated life.

I rub the green grub from my eyelids and mutter obscenities about evil makeup pushers as we leave the store. Lauren giggles, and we step out into the blinding Arizona sun. We agree—oddly, in a way only two women who have shared a beauty ritual can—that perhaps subjugation depends on your point of view. Consider Randy. Consider Lindsay, Paris, and Britney. Consider the thousands of American high-school students taking a sex-ed class that suggests the only thing you need to know about sex is how not to have it. For now, ours is a confused culture in a free country. Lauren and I find our car and, burning our fingertips on the hot metal, unlock it. Soon, to the tune of the Kelly Clarkson song, I mentally sing, "Go forth and search for love any way you can."

An Open Letter to the Bush Administration
Mistress Morgana Maye

San Francisco, California

My name is Morgana Maye, and I'm a small business owner living and working in San Francisco. I appreciate that your administration strives to "create an environment where entrepreneurs can flourish," but I'm writing today because, despite the president's assertion that small business is "the heart of the American economy," your agenda has adversely affected my business as a professional dominatrix. I've examined my business plan, my advertising, and the trend toward neoconservative sex negativity, but I keep coming back to the same gut feeling: you're doing my job better than I can.

If wartime is good for prostitutes and lap dancers, it's hell on dominatrices. The professional dominatrix makes her money for the same reason disaster movies make millions: people love to be subjected to their greatest fears while remaining realistically safe.

Production studios understand this. They will delay the release of movies about terrorist plots or natural disasters when such events have actually occurred. They know there is something in the consumer conscience that feels guilty about being entertained by misery and destruction.

My work deals with the sexual fantasy of disempowerment. Fantasy is a tricky artifice. It relies, in part, on the assurance of impossibility. The same fantastical impulse that draws millions into movie theaters to watch zombies destroy the world brings men into my dungeon where they can enact a fantasy of their utter destruction without any real danger of being harmed. It's cathartic, it's entertaining, it cuts through all the bourgeois comfort of being white and male and landed, without actually subverting any of the comforts of being white and male and landed.

I explain all of this to you because over the past seven years your administration has successfully organized what has to be longest nonconsensual public edge-play scene in recent history. I look at your capacity to manufacture fear, degradation, torture, and absolute powerlessness, and I can't top that. Your current policy of world domination is so excessive, it dwarfs any attempt by an independent contractor, like myself, to do so on a more person-by-person basis.

I have a better international travel record than Mr. Bush, a stronger right arm than Mr. Rumsfeld, and a better rack than Ms. Rice, but I don't have anything close to your operating budget, and I adhere to a code of ethics and social responsibility that prevents me from competing with you on any real level. I was at the top of my field, a seasoned sadist and skilled edge player with more than a decade of experience, yet over the past seven years your campaign has rendered me a Pollyanna by comparison. You are bad for my corporate image, and are disenfranchising me from the American Dream of profitable small business ownership.

It's not just that you're marketing yourself as a bigger, badder top. You're taking the fantasy out of torture and domination and making it real, which is triggering that annoying consumer conscience and driving away my clients. The week the Abu Ghraib prison scandal broke and pictures of naked, bound, hooded men were splashed on the cover of every magazine and on every newscast the world over, I had two extended sessions booked consisting of twelve hours of heavy electro-genitorture, full sensory deprivation, and humiliating interrogation. One client canceled outright, saying it just didn't feel right and that he was going to reexamine why he was "into all this stuff" anyway; the other asked if I could conduct the session in any room other than the dungeon, perhaps a kitchen where he could wear a frilly dress and wash my floor, and just feel "safe" for a few hours.

Your policies have stripped the sexiness out of being inescapably imprisoned for no reason and with no due process. In fact, the only subgroup of my clientele that has increased over the past seven years has been adult babies. You've reduced the world to a place where people just want to cuddle and hear a bedtime story. This is hardly an apt use of my skills or equipment, and certainly not a broad enough clientele for me to make my house payment.

And if your out-domming me and driving away my clients isn't enough of a complaint, I'd like to point out that the professional dominatrix bases her sessions on the doctrine of preemptive strike. This whole policy of "I'm going to punish you before you've been bad" is so my shtick. I was employing preemptive strike before Mr. Bush's daddy was in office the first time around; I have a published precedent. If shticks were copyright protected, I'd sue and retire to the Bahamas on my settlement.

I'm not asking for a lot, but as a taxpayer and an American,

I have a couple of requests. You could stop advertising, for one thing. Previous administrations did a much better job of keeping their agenda for world domination on the down low. Besides, tops that tout themselves as ruthlessly as you do, especially in the face of bad reviews, always strike me as distastefully insecure. And since it's doubtful in this era of self-imposed antitrust policy, how about a subsidy, or federal grant to compensate me for profits lost due to the unfair expenditure of $255 million dollars a day in Iraq? That comes out to about $10.6 million dollars per hours, or $177,000 per minute. For the cost of about five minutes of your time in Iraq I could pay off my mortgage and have a nice little nest egg for myself. I'll get out of the business and leave your number on my voice mail as a referral for my clients.

Respectfully Yours,
Mistress Morgana Maye

The Pleasure of Unpleasure
Kristina Lloyd

All writers get bad reviews; if you write erotica, your sexuality gets reviewed as well. Trust me, you sometimes need a thick skin to deal with this. We are all, as individuals, never more vulnerable than when we reveal our desiring selves to others, and smut writers do this on a grand scale. Sure, it's framed within a fiction and no one can see us blush. But with that distance comes a space which allows strangers to pass judgment.

Here are a few things that have been said about me. I mean, about my books:

Most of the sex scenes are degrading—not arousing.

Great if you like the idea of being humiliated and called slut etc., not so great if you don't.

Ilya is a man who truly doesn't respect Beth in the least, doesn't even like her.

You would think that an erotic fiction book would be at least a little bit sensual.

I pitied Beth more than I wanted to be in her place.

One of the worst Black Lace books I have ever read.

I found some of the BDSM disgusting.

Nothing against a kinky read but I don't like mental abuse in erotic books.

Ouch!

My grumble isn't really with negative comments; I think it's par for the course when you're a writer. And, I'm pleased to report, they're vastly outnumbered by the very many positive, insightful, considered reviews my work has received over the years.

No, my problem is with the way erotic humiliation is so frequently misunderstood, reviled, and marginalized. I write a lot about women who get off on being used, degraded, and verbally dominated; about rape fantasy; about discomfort, conflict, fear. Pain isn't my kink. Spanking is off my radar. Rough stuff and psychological humiliation is more my theme although, of course, the physical and the mental don't form neat parcels for anyone. When I write about this and someone says "Ew! Gross!," they're saying that what turns me on is wrong.

An editor once reminded me that erotic fiction needs to focus on pleasure rather than be a vehicle for dysfunction. I was so stunned by this I didn't eat worms for the rest of the week and almost quit my basket-weaving. I am not dysfunctional. I am not damaged. And what on earth is "pleasure" anyway? It sounds suspiciously like scented candles to me. The notion that female erotica should be softer and more romantic is wildly offensive. Ditto the implication that a woman who wants to be dominated by a man must be lacking her own mind. *She* doesn't want it. She's merely a victim and it's her damaged, self-loathing psyche talking. Oh, puhlease.

I get a lot of pleasure from unpleasure, from being made to squirm, from hating it and loving it all at once. All those who are with me, say "Ay!" One of the most moving erotic scenes I've ever read is in Stephen Elliott's *My Girlfriend Comes to the City and Beats Me Up*. The narrator, a male submissive new to the BDSM scene, after hours of being tied, gagged, hurt, and demeaned is fucked with a strap-on. Elliott writes:

> I had never been entered before. She leaned across my back, wrapping one arm around my chest and gripping my neck with her other hand, occasionally squeezing my windpipe so I couldn't breathe for a second. I cried again, but it was a different crying. I was very comfortable. I don't think I had ever been comfortable before.

"Comfortable" might seem an odd word to use in this context but I think it's perfect. For me, it's that sense of dreamy, egoless relief that arises in the tension between pleasure and unpleasure. Subspace, to use the jargon. A lot of my characters (jeez, I can't think who they're based on) get off on being treated badly, on being distressed, reduced, shamed, and scared. They're not screwballs, nihilists, emotional masochists, or lacking in self-worth. It's a sex thang. They can still function.

Beth, my central character in *Asking for Trouble,* is a woman exploring her taste for sleaze, danger, submission, and humiliation. Ilya is the enigmatic stranger she's newly involved with. She confesses her fantasies to him: "I just like picturing things where I'm being used, objectified, degraded, that kind of stuff. It's liberating. I'm in someone else's hands. I'm not being me."

Once upon a time, academics wrote about Black Lace books and the new phenomenon of women writing porn. One academic, analyzing *Asking for Trouble*, quoted the above dialogue and said, "So once again then, we see in the woman who liberates her sexuality and embraces eroticism the simultaneous flight from selfhood."

Huh? Flight from selfhood? Isn't half the point of sex the way in which we can transcend ourselves? (What's the other half? Someone remind me? Oh, yes: cock.) In *Split*, my spooky puppets-and-bondage novel, I explore what submission and degradation mean a little bit more. Kate is falling in love with Jake, the strange and beautiful curator of an isolated puppet museum in the Yorkshire Moors. She's gradually coming to understand how the power imbalance of their sexual relationship fulfills her:

> He breaks me down, strips me of inhibitions, and when I've sobbed and climaxed until I don't know who I am, he wraps me in his arms, so soft and tender.
>
> Do I sound like a masochist? I don't feel like one. The point isn't the pain and I don't suffer. Or rather, I go beyond suffering and into a new space. If I could get there without it hurting, I would. I think that's why I like it when Jake calls me 'slut' and makes me feel bad. It takes me there, helps me lose myself [...] and it's as if I'm in a nothing space, floating. I am so free there.
>
> It's such a feeling to be free of yourself. I didn't understand it at first. I think it scared me but I'm getting to know and understand it. I'm coming to realize that I want this not

because I'm worthless and I must suffer. It's because I'm human and life's tough. Letting go is so powerful. Surrender transforms me. I adore oblivion.

Kate, like Beth, is a woman conflicted about her sexuality. I think this is true of a lot of people whose kinks are on the dark side, and I think this is okay. We hear a lot about "sex positivity" and having a "healthy" attitude; and while I applaud the sentiment it leaves me feeling a tad uncomfortable. It seems so neat, clean, and tidy, and leaves little space for angst or doubt. Where we want to go and what we want to do or be done to us can be disturbing, terrifying, upsetting, and exciting. It's pleasure but not as they know it. Accepting conflict and contradiction is a significant part of accepting our messy sexual selves. I'm sure "sex positive" was originally meant to encompass this but it's easily miscast to imply unproblematic happy-jolly-fucky sex. It can make me feel dirty, and not in a good way.

I like brutes and bullies with a nice line in contempt. I like back alleys, seediness, and squalor. I like scary scenarios that make my heart beat faster. All these things break down the ego and strip away the veneer of the civilized self. And when you're without that constructed identity, when your dignity and self-respect have been put on hold, then boundaries shift, inhibitions are lost. If anything, those who like to indulge in being broken down need to have a very secure sense of self. They must be continually piecing themselves back together again afterward.

I imagine a scene. To some eyes, it may look like a woman on her knees in a crack den, sobbing in shame with her hair full of piss, being mocked by a couple of thugs. But for plenty of people, suffering and degradation is intensely erotic. It's the pleasure of unpleasure, of being split between yes and no. I like it there. I'm comfortable. The scented candles can go hang!

What's "Normal" Sex?

Brian Alexander

This month the American Psychiatric Association announced the names of "working group" members who will guide the development of the new *Diagnostic and Statistical Manual of Mental Disorders,* or *DSM,* the codex of American psychiatry.

Not surprisingly, given the *DSM's* colorful history, particularly when it comes to sex, controversy erupted within days of the announcement, especially over membership of the Sexual and Gender Identity Disorders working group, which will wrestle with questions such as: Are sadomasochism or pedophilia mental disorders? Are dysfunctions like female hypoactive sexual desire disorder (low sex drive) psychiatric issues, or hormonal issues? Perhaps the most important question is whether, when it comes to many sexual interests and issues, it's even possible or desirable to create diagnostic criteria.

At least one petition, spearheaded by transgender activists, is being circulated to oppose the appointment of some members to the Sexual and Gender Identity Disorders work group and its chair, Kenneth Zucker, head of the Gender Identity Service at the Center for Addiction and Mental Health in Toronto, Canada. The petition accuses Zucker of having engaged in "junk science" and promoting "hurtful theories" during his career, especially advocating the idea that children who are unambiguously male or female anatomically, but seem confused about their gender identity, can be treated by encouraging gender expression in line with their anatomy.

Zucker rejects the junk-science charge, saying that there "has to be an empirical basis to modify anything" in the *DSM*. As for hurting people, "in my own career, my primary motivation in working with children, adolescents, and families is to help them with the distress and suffering they are experiencing, whatever the reasons they are having these struggles. I want to help people feel better about themselves, not hurt them."

That sex is controversial comes as no surprise to Dr. Darrel Regier, the vice-chair of the APA's *DSM-V* Task Force, based in Arlington, Virginia.

Sex, he says, in an understatement, "is an area that obviously has lots of emotion attached to it." But the APA, he says, is doing its best to put science and evidence first, both in who it appoints to working groups and in the process it will use to create the *DSM-V* (so called because it is the fifth complete version). Each working group will accept input from many experts with varying views, reach a consensus on *DSM* content, and then put that work group's product before the board of trustees of the APA and the APA assembly.

All that may be true, but Regier does not expect such reassurances to quell the forces already swirling around the *DSM-V* as it moves toward a 2012 publication date. Currently, the *DSM-IV* includes sex-related activities as varied as paraphilias like voyeurism, klismaphilia (erotic use of enemas), and sadism, and functional disorders like dyspareunia (pain with intercourse), erectile disorders, and premature ejaculation.

"A Set of Scientific Hypotheses"

The first *DSM* was issued in 1952. The idea was to create a more standardized way of talking about psychiatric disorders. As psychiatrist Dr. Gail Saltz, a "Today Show" contributor who also practices in New York, explains, the *DSM* is best viewed as "a language we have chosen to speak, a talking point we mental health professionals have created to communicate as well as we can with each other and with other professions."

It is not a final arbiter of who's crazy and who's not. Saltz, who says she thinks the *DSM* can be limiting in clinical practice, prefers to take a holistic approach and look at each patient's collection of symptoms and concerns without being restricted by the *DSM*'s various criteria.

Regier agrees that's how doctors should use it, arguing that the *DSM* "really needs to be seen as a set of scientific hypotheses." It is, he believes, "a living document" changeable with new research.

But if the *DSM* is a book of "hypotheses," why the fuss? Does the *DSM* matter?

Yes. A lot.

The first reason why is prosaic. If you want your insurance to reimburse your visit to a mental health professional, you are probably going to need a *DSM* code signifying a diagnosis.

But the more profound reason is that it shapes how doctors, and even the rest of society, view sexuality.

"A psychiatric diagnosis is more than shorthand to facilitate communication among professionals or to standardize research parameters," wrote Dr. Charles Moser and Peggy Kleinplatz in a 2005 paper published in the *Journal of Psychology and Human Sexuality*. "Psychiatric diagnoses affect child custody decisions, self-esteem, whether individuals are hired or fired, receive security clearances, or have other rights and privileges curtailed. Criminals may find that their sentences are either mitigated or enhanced as a direct result of their diagnoses. The equating of unusual sexual interests with psychiatric diagnoses has been used to justify the oppression of sexual minorities and to serve political agendas. A review of this area is not only a scientific issue, but also a human rights issue."

A Problem for Whom?

There is no shortage of opinion on what ought to be changed, deleted, or included in the new *DSM-V.* Sandra Leiblum, formerly a professor at New Jersey's Robert Wood Johnson Medical School and an expert in female sexual health who is now in private practice in Bridgewater, New Jersey, says she wants to see a revision of diagnoses of female hypoactive sexual desire disorder, other female arousal disorders, and sexual pain like dyspareunia. For example, she wants language that would separate arousal disorders into genital (more biological in origin) and subjective subtypes.

Carol Queen, a sexologist, sexual rights activist, and cofounder of San Francisco's Center for Sex and Culture, believes the new *DSM* should stress that sexual variances are only a problem "if they are problems in the life of the person showing up" in a psychiatrist's office "so that when somebody is eroticizing something, or doing something in a consensual way, that's not a problem" even if it may seem odd to most of us.

She also proposes an addition, a diagnosis of "absexual" ("ab" meaning "away from"). This would include those who appear to be "turned on by fulminating against it." Examples could include state governors who crusade against prostitution even while paying hookers for sex, and religious leaders who wind up trying to explain engaging in the sex acts they preach against.

Moser, who is affiliated with the Institute for Advanced Study of Human Sexuality in San Francisco, and Kleinplatz, from the University of Ottawa, argue that all paraphilias, like sexual sadism, sexual masochism, and transvestism, should be removed from the *DSM,* insisting that "the *DSM* criteria for diagnosis of unusual sexual interests as pathological rests on a series of unproven and more importantly, untested assumptions."

This does not mean, as opponents of this idea have suggested, that they somehow approve of sex between adults and children. "We would argue that the removal of pedophilia from the *DSM* would focus attention on the criminal aspect of these acts, and not allow the perpetrators to claim mental illness as a defense or use it to mitigate responsibility for their crimes," they wrote. "Individuals convicted of these crimes should be punished as provided by the laws in the jurisdiction in which the crime occurred."

Most of these suggestions are inherently political, as much as the APA and most psychiatrists would wish to avoid politics. Sex exists as part of the culture, and it cannot be separated from it.

The *DSM* has reflected cultural shifts through its revisions and new editions. The most famous example is homosexuality. When the first *DSM* was created in 1952, homosexuality was declared a mental illness. By 1973, and after much heated debate and over objections from religious conservatives, the *DSM-II* excluded homosexuality as a disorder with the exception of one variant, and that was soon dropped in an interim revision.

Once Deviant, Now Desirable

"Definitely a change in culture affects diagnoses," Leiblum says. "We used to think oral-genital sex was deviant and we have embraced that. Masturbation was evidence of out-of-control behavior; now we see it as not only normative but to be encouraged."

So if enough people start to do it, or are more public about doing it, does that mean it is no longer a disorder? "I think it probably affects the degree to which people are willing to look at scientific evidence," Regier says.

This fuzziness is why, starting in the 1980s, the field moved toward adding the notion of "distress" to the *DSM*.

"We do not consider something a disorder unless there is a clearly defined description of this entity and there is clearly some significant dysfunction and distress associated with it," explains Regier. "I would say also if there is no victim involved... this behavior is not imposing a person's will on another person, that is a critical component when one looks at conditions in this area."

If you aren't distressed, and everyone is a consenting grown-up, then there probably isn't a disorder. But things won't be that simple for the creators of the new *DSM*.

"How do you make a criteria that does not pathologize low desire?" Leiblum asks rhetorically. You add the need to be distressed about it. "But then whose distress should be looked at?" she asks, referring to a sexual partner. "You can have hypertension and not feel any distress because there is objective criteria for what is high blood pressure. But there is none of that for sexual diagnoses, even premature ejaculation. What constitutes premature?"

(At a press conference Monday, the International Society of Sexual Medicine made a stab at a definition, saying premature ejaculation is "a male sexual dysfunction characterized by ejaculation which always or nearly always occurs prior to or within about one minute of vaginal penetration; and, inability to delay ejaculation on all or nearly all vaginal penetrations; and, negative personal consequences, such as distress, bother, frustration, and/or the avoidance of sexual intimacy.")

This problematic lack of clarity, Leiblum argues, is especially acute for the paraphilias. Does the criteria amount to "If it's mine it's okay, but if it's yours it's kinky? These issues need to be grappled with."

Unleash the Beast

"Josephine Thomas"

I am faithful to my husband for 2,292 days. But on the 2,293rd day, I have hormonal teenage sex with a veritable stranger in his divorced-bachelor pad by the train tracks. I've slept with some sixty men over two decades and yet it's with this middle-aged man—graying, with wrinkles and soft muscles—that I truly discover sex.

He is a stranger, but we have a history. One day two years ago, we sat next to each other on the commuter bus, chatting, flirting. I found him incredibly sexy. Our thighs touched in a way that suggested it wasn't a coincidence. I fantasized about him a good deal in the following weeks. I imagined that, engrossed in conversation, I'd miss my stop, and he'd offer, like a gentleman, to drive me home once we got to his place. Of course we'd have incredibly hot, animalistic sex on his enclosed sunporch, and there'd be nothing gentlemanly about it.

Now, all this time later, I am waiting one morning for the commuter train when I see him walk onto the platform. He comes straight over to me, smiling broadly, as if we're old friends. He's just come from the chiropractor because he hurt his back. He looks good. He remembers my name. I learn within minutes that he's separated from his wife and is living a couple of blocks away. He neglects to mention that he has a steady girlfriend because, consciously or not, he knows what I know: We're going to fuck. Soon.

The fact that I don't feel one ounce guilty about contemplating adultery should make me feel like a coldhearted sociopath, but it doesn't. The plain truth is that I've had a problem with fidelity all my romantic life. I was never faithful to any of my boyfriends. I would cheat on current boyfriends with new ones, on new ones with exes. I once left a lover in my bed for a dalliance with another, then came back as if I'd just run down to the store for milk. In fact, infidelity is a pastime of which I am rather fond, a behavior that I tamped down when I exchanged vows with my husband but that I never truly buried.

The moment I see train-station man, with his impish grin, I am instantly my good old, bad old self again. Maybe it's because he turned up after a long, tedious spell of monogamy. Maybe it's because childbirth deeply wounded my body image, and his flattery is just the balm to soothe it. It's also possible that I'm more resentful than I realize of my husband, who refuses to take a turn getting up early with the kids on weekends because he's so tired from doing the very important job that pays for our really nice house. Whatever the reason, train-station man manages not only to revive my mischievous, affair-loving streak, but ultimately to open me up to something that is, oddly enough, new to me: the exquisite joy of sex.

His first email, later that day—after the train doesn't show and he gives me a lift into the city—is fairly innocent but suggestive enough if I choose to take the bait:

What a treat to see you waiting for the train this morning. I thought it would be nice to talk to you for a few minutes before it arrived. Little did I know I would get to have you all to myself for an entire car ride into the city. Now I'm glad I hurt my back. :)

I feel no shame or fear in pursuing this, only pure adrenaline-pumped pleasure. I know exactly where it's going to lead because that's where I want it to lead. I admit in my reply to him that I wasn't able to concentrate much at my meeting since my mind was "elsewhere." This time he takes the bait and writes back:

I remember very well the feeling of sitting so close to you on the bus and the pull you describe. And, to tell you the truth, I thought about it yesterday when we walked to get my car. I imagined asking you to come upstairs with me for a minute so I could get something I'd forgotten. You are ahead of me on the stairs and we're making small talk as we walk. The sound of our footsteps and our breathing is echoing slightly in the hallway, but otherwise the building is quiet. Most everyone has gone to work already.

As we start up the last flight before my door, you stop and turn toward me to make a joke about something I just said. I don't stop, though. I keep walking until I'm on the step below you. You pause for a second because I'm standing so close, and the atmosphere changes. Suddenly things are very electric, and the sound of our breathing is now quite pronounced.

My right hand is on the banister, but my left slides up the wall and comes to rest, very lightly, on your hip. I never take my eyes off yours, but my hand moves slowly around the small of your back and pulls you in a little closer. I lean in and place my lips so that they are almost touching your neck, just below the jawline. You can feel my breath warm against your skin, while my other hand grazes your hip and comes to rest on the back of your other leg, just below the hem of your skirt, and slides slowly up and stops just at the point where it meets your...

The emails quickly cross the line from PG to R, and then NC-17. They reach such a frenzy that a rendezvous is all but inevitable, and about twenty-four hours later, I am in his apartment, naked, my legs wrapped around his torso, his strong arms guiding my body up and down on his. It's amazing. He's amazing. I haven't felt this alive in years.

It's possible that I've had other great lovers before, but that I was too young to fully appreciate their prowess, or maybe I was too distracted by my ulterior motive—the conquest itself—to relax and enjoy. Or maybe it's just that train-station man is more experienced and more confident in bed than any man I've ever been with, so he understands what women need. I do know that he's an extremely generous lover, and that he genuinely wants to give—it's not just a ruse to get to intercourse faster.

Even if the sex weren't stellar, which it is, the ego trip is out of this world.

Here I am, approaching forty. I've had two kids, one by C-section, with a nasty scar to prove it. My breasts have fallen, my hips have widened; I've got grandma arms and saddlebags. And yet here is this very attractive man, well into his forties, beholding my naked body in wonderment as if I'm a Victoria's Secret model, no, make that the Botticelli *Venus* herself, landed on his futon, a gift from heaven. His hands trace the curves up and down my body. He tells me I'm an incredibly tasty thing, hot and sexy and interesting and compelling. I'm addicted.

Why don't I feel guilty? In part, I blame my upbringing; the daughter of a very public figure, I always seemed exempt from the rules everyone else had to follow. My parents, overachievers themselves and dead set on impressing the world, encouraged me to take shortcuts, to use connections to get things first or more easily, cheaper or faster. If I did the conventional thing, if I actually filled out a job or school application and sent it off cold to an anonymous person, or walked into a store and bought something retail, I was not being clever, not using every resource to my advantage. And nothing succeeded like success. The message was clear: achieve your goal. The subtext was even clearer: whatever it takes. With each success, I lapped up my parents' praise and then got greedy for more.

Somehow that need for praise and attention translated into sexual conquest. I found, well before puberty, that getting boys to notice me provided the same gratification. By age fourteen, I was a raging slut, seducing boys at school, at camp, in the neighborhood. Every encounter left me high. It was like crack.

For many years I believed I had an insatiable appetite for sex, but whenever I was in a committed relationship, it lost its appeal almost entirely. No, for me sex was about the invincible power I could wield over the opposite sex. And the more illicit the encounter, the better: in a coatroom, in a kiddie pool, on a stage in a darkened theater after hours. I loved feeling I was getting away with something, getting it first or more easily, cheaper or faster.

I slept with so many men that the only way I can remember them is to go through the alphabet, making allowances for those nameless conquests—bouncer at the Ritz, American University senior at the beach, the DJ who got me an autographed Madonna album. When I finally settled down at age twenty-eight, it wasn't so much that I'd found my sexual match as that I'd found other qualities to value. We played Scrabble and did crossword puzzles together; we liked the same bands. Neither of us ever carried a balance on a credit card. He liked when I cooked for him; he loved how I looked in a miniskirt. We got along swimmingly, effortlessly. He'd had his share of conquests too. I felt understood. I had a best friend. I was happy.

Fast-forward ten years. I'm working from my home in the sub-urbs to be close to my two kids. I hardly ever see my husband, who's gone for some thirteen hours on weekdays, and I hardly see men other than my husband, let alone sexy ones or, even more unimaginable, sexy ones who undress me with their eyes. I feel old, invisible, practically dead. I hired a fairly attractive exterminator once, but then he cleaned up bat shit in my attic and I lost my very mild interest. The closest I ever got to flirting now was with the cute fathers who occasionally picked up their kids at my daughter's preschool. And that's when the beast inside me—the one that once fed voraciously off male attention—roused from its hibernation long enough for me to feel a flicker of adrenaline, a pang for my glory days as a wild seductress of men. Then it usually sighed, curled up, and went back to sleep.

Not this time. On this day I allow the beast, ravenous from years of starvation, to come roaring back to life. I don't even try to quiet it. I send train-station man another email, and it's practically pornographic:

> I swear I've been totally WET now for days, just from periodic—okay, nearly constant—thinking about your electrifying sexuality. In fact, I actually think my nether

regions are kind of swollen from all the excitement. Is that possible?

He replies:

> God, I am so fucking hard thinking about your sweet little body and the things I want to do to it that I can barely concentrate on anything else. I didn't tell you this, but that day on the bus, I was slouched down in my seat (so I could feel like I was closer to you) and I was fantasizing about doing things to you, like fucking you with my fingers, and you would have to keep really quiet so the bus driver wouldn't know.

I know that what I'm doing is wrong, but I know it only on an academic level. Inside, I don't care. I can't care. It feels too good. It feels like home. I feel like me again, awash in the euphoria of a new relationship and drunk with the power I'm thrilled to realize I still have. And this time it's not over a pimply teen or a brooding college student but over a fully grown man (who, as such, should know better). I get him to leave work early, to duck out of his son's birthday party, to lie to the people he loves just to see me. It's not that I'm mean. It's that I'm addicted—to the ego boost, certainly, but also, perhaps for the first time, to the sex itself.

After the birth of my second child, I cried the first few times I slept with my husband because I just felt so undesirable, like he was sleeping with me out of pity. Poor fat Josie with a nasty scar and a pouchy belly. He told me, charitably, that he "didn't find me unattractive" but his soft dick proved otherwise. We had sex pretty infrequently after that, occasionally noticing a month or more had passed since our last conjugal visit. The frequency picked up slightly over the following year and a half, but at some point during his pushing and grunting, long after I'd lost any lubrication I was able to achieve, I would count the seconds until it was over. Sex began taking place only in the middle of the night when, half-asleep, my husband would get turned on by our spooning and begin clumsily removing my pajamas. I considered it a new low.

Train-station man, with his alabaster skin and pool blue eyes, changes all that by giving me something I so desperately need— permission to accept and even embrace my body. He writes:

> It was delicious doing all the things to you that I had envisioned beforehand, especially approaching you from all different angles. And take it from me: your extremely hot body looks good from any angle. My personal favorites so far are you on top of me, head thrown back, eyes closed, riding me; you standing, hands against the wall, half turned back to look at me while I put my hands all over you; you lying naked on your side, back to me, while I stroke and caress you, then slip my finger slowly inside you.
>
> I keep wanting to come over there and throw you down on any available surface and take you, again and again and again…

What amazes me most is that this man didn't know me when I was young and nubile with perky breasts and flat abs, so that now he might merely be looking past the ravages of time and childbirth. This man is attracted to the woman I am now, warts and all. And though his emails have slowed to a trickle and become more perfunctory (*Okay then, see you at three*), the legacy of the affair remains very much alive, even affecting the way I take care of myself: I'm shaving my legs more often, applying face masks, actually flossing. I'm wearing makeup most days, even with no plans to leave the house, and I've joined the gym.

The fourth time I sleep with train-station man, the thrill is beginning to wear off. He's still amazing in bed, but the fireworks are gone. We're just two grown-up people enjoying a fine afternoon fuck. And as I descend the three flights to the parking lot behind his building, I wonder if it will be for the last time.

I also realize it almost doesn't matter. I've already reaped an incredible, unforeseen reward from this affair: far from detracting from my sex life at home, it has significantly improved it—and, by extension, my relationship with my husband—simply by making me feel desirable again and by showing me how much fun sex can be. This affair has been like a giant "aha" moment that's enriched my life beyond belief. It's as though he has helped me become a citizen of the sexual world, and it's a wonderful place to be.

Will sex with my husband ever trump or even match the magical lovemaking I've been enjoying with train-station man? Probably not. But is it better than it's been in a long time? Absolutely. I feel freer to talk dirty, to guide his hands, to show off my body instead of hiding it under the covers. My newfound confidence has rekindled his desire too, adding more fuel to the sexual fire. Better still, we're doing crossword puzzles again. We're eating dinner together and actually talking—the very things that tamed the sex fiend in me in the first place. Just yesterday he downloaded two CDs' worth of my favorite songs and presented them to me as a gift. We're getting back to being involved in each other's lives in that simple, loving way. And that's a huge dividend from an illicit affair with a gray-haired stranger I met at the train station.

Is Cybersex Cheating?
Violet Blue

"Hey. Baby. I know you like to have some fun. You. Know. Where to find me," burbles Kari, the Virtual Girlfriend in a halting, female Stephen Hawking voice through my G4's speakers. But while Kari might be the most advanced commercially available artificial intelligence pleasure model online, if I walked in on a boyfriend having an 8-bit roll in the hay with her, I'd be fighting the urge to laugh, not the urge to throw dishes. Cybersex, it seems, might just be in the eye of the beholder.

Right now there are more ways to have cybersex than ever thought possible, and it's making modern couples reconfigure their relationships' Terms of Service. Cybersex makes it easy to cheat; you don't have to meet anyone, so the risk factor is low on all fronts—except maybe emotionally. Cybersex is also a more creative form of masturbation, so in many ways it's not too terribly different than enjoying porn or fantasy. But that cybersex often involves another human gives it a twist; walking in on a boyfriend with an actual human female on the other side of the screen, having a hot and heavy text or cam session—I don't need to consult our ToS to know that wouldn't feel good, at all.

But if it's really just masturbation, then is cybersex "real" sex? Dr. Keely Kolmes, PsyD, a San Francisco psychotherapist for individuals and couples, tells me, "I would say that whether or not it is 'real' sex depends upon how the interaction is experienced by the participants. It may even feel 'real' for one person in the encounter, and not for the other person with whom they are having cybersex. On the other hand, you may have two people having cybersex where neither of them considers it 'real,' despite arousal, a feeling of intimacy, and even mutual orgasm—and yet their real-life partners may beg to differ." Kolmes adds, "But it's fascinating that two people can be having an experience and one person may compartmentalize it in a way that feels 'not real,' while the other person is feeling much more integrated about it."

For Ellie Lumpesse (lumpesse.com), it's sex all right—and thank goodness, because that's what she and her committed, live-in boyfriend of three years are openly looking for. She occasionally engages in cybersex with multiple partners on her own, and sometimes the couple has a cyber "threesome." The techno-poly couple is up front that the status of their relationship is nonmonogamous, but I still wondered how this nouveau poly arrangement negotiated the murky waters of cybersex and infidelity. Lumpesse explains, "Cheating is an interesting question. In my relationship we are incredibly open and honest. We don't have many rules, so there isn't much to lie about. Really, the only rule we have is to share what we are feeling and planning. So, for me, infidelity is taking an action or having a feeling that I think my partner would want to know but that I'm not telling him for some reason. I used to say that I 'don't do anything I wouldn't want him sitting next to me while I'm doing,' but I think that is pretty reductive and too prone to literal interpretation. Instead, any sort of keeping secrets feels like infidelity to me."

To Kolmes, this makes a lot of sense; cybersex outside a non-monogamous relationship is a natural fit. "These kinds of different conceptions of the same sexual acts are not new for poly couples who may have very different feelings about various sensual, emotional, or sexual activities (i.e., the relative intimacy of kissing, versus more genital-specific touching, versus BDSM play, et cetera)." How this might work, Kolmes explains, "Some people may draw the line at cybersex with known people, saying that this would feel like too much of a violation, and that it's only okay if their partner plays with (presumed) strangers. Others may feel better having clear rules about sharing the logs of the activity. Some may want to watch or supervise. Some may prefer that the cybersex be around particular acts that are less appealing to them (fantasy play or sex acts that the partner may not enjoy as much). Others may feel more comfortable if their partner has cybersex using some other identity (gender role switching, or via a virtual avatar, in a game, or whatever)."

But there's being okay with it, and there's…not. We've all read the *Cosmo* articles about the fiancée who walked in on her almost-husband with his mouse in one hand and his—mouse—in the other, shockingly busting him having cybersex. (Yes, you read it. Continue.) To her this is a transgression, although it's likely not a clear one; it hurts; she feels jealous, betrayed, lied to, cheated on, and generally wonders if she's enough for him. But cybersex is layered and sometimes mysterious and complex. Unless he explains what's going on, it's tough to determine if it's healthy fantasy and masturbation (that is, if she's even okay with that concept), or having an actual sexual—or emotional—affair with another girl. He might have it tucked away in the "it's not about my real relationship" area of his psyche, but for her it is. The difficulty with cybersex and monogamy, besides explaining sticky keyboards, is knowing when a line's been crossed.

How do you know if you're crossing a cybersex line? Talking about your cybersexuality with your partner is the right thing to do, but yeah, like that's easy when it's been an ongoing thing, or you have a fetish you don't know how (or want) to share. But if you're monogamous and having cybersex with someone who's not your partner, you need to know how to tell when the line's been crossed. Some advise that if it feels like cheating, it likely is. But Kolmes reminds us that it isn't that cut and dried, helpfully advising what to look for. "Signs that you may be crossing a line would include things like feeling guilty about it or feeling the need to keep it a secret. Or if you find that you're using cybersex as a safe way to express specific fantasies with someone that you are afraid to share with your relationship partner(s). Complaining about your relationship to the person you're engaging in cybersex with or using it in some way to devalue your relationship would also be signs that you are crossing boundaries. Canceling out on other face-to-face engagements with people in your life in order to have cybersex could be a bad sign."

For better or for worse, there is no restart or reload for relationships; once you find yourself through the looking glass of cybersex and possible (or actual) violation of your relationship's ToS, it's time to talk. Kolmes suggests, "If you want to start talking about cybersex after you may have crossed some boundaries, it might be good to start by talking about fantasies and other erotic supplements to your fantasy life (such as pictures, videos, written erotica, toys)." Just talking about sex in general, Kolmes says, "would be a good launching point for acknowledging that there haven't been conversations about using more interactive media or involving other live people. If these types of conversations feel too intimidating, or they are not going well, it might be useful to consider getting help from a sex-positive therapist who works with people in relationships. It is also important to find a therapist who won't jump directly to assuming that this is a case of porn addiction or Internet addiction—but to find someone who can help you and your partner communicate more explicitly about fantasy, desires, and about how to talk about these things."

However, not everyone is going to be wigged out by a little on-line canoodling. Some might think it's kinda hot, or even a new sex toy for the couple to share and add to the buffet of sexual activities the couple already enjoys. For these couples, Lumpesse speaks from experience when it comes to surfing the cybersex seas from within a relationship. "I probably have more than one piece of advice for couples," she adds. "The obvious one is that nonmonogamy is like anal sex. If you protect yourself, go slow, and communicate a lot, it can be amazing. If you don't, OUCH! The other thing I would tell people to consider is that jealousy might not be the most impor-tant emotion they ever have. I still get jealous all the time; I've just learned that it is a fleeting response, and I don't have to let it dictate my actions and decisions."

That said, we'll see how things go when I take the Virtual Boy-friend for a test drive. If I don't have any dishes left, I'll be reshelv-ing my copy of *A Brief History of Time* with the rest of the erotica.

Sex Offenders!!

Kelly Davis

Most people reading this will remember when there were no public sex-offender registries—no online portals where you can type in your address and find out if a sex offender is living nearby or sign up to receive an email alert when one moves into your neighborhood. A decade ago, there weren't folks who memorized names and faces and went door-to-door to let their neighbors know that a sex offender had moved in down the street—no one putting up fliers in apartment-building lobbies and laundry rooms.

No sex-offender registry or neighborhood watch would have kept a babysitter from molesting me when I was six. He was around sixteen or seventeen, the brother of our regular babysitter who filled in whenever his sister was busy. I don't remember how many times it happened, but I know it was more than once. Years later, I found out that he molested my sister, who was four, and my best friend, who lived across the street.

At some point I told my mom what happened, but I don't know what words I used. At six, "penis," "vagina," and "sex" weren't part of my vocabulary. Whatever I said, my mom didn't believe me—at least that's what she told me.

Looking back, I think she knew I was telling the truth, but she just didn't know how to respond.

And then I simply forgot that it ever happened—until my first serious relationship in high school, when I had to admit to the guy that, in my mind, the male penis was a diseased, disgusting thing. A year later I ended up in counseling for severe anxiety and depression. There was a box on a questionnaire asking if I'd ever been the victim of sexual abuse, and that opened the door.

A couple of weeks ago, I threw the babysitter's name into a national sexual-offender registry. A match came up, but the photo was a guy from Texas who happened to have the same name. I doubt the babysitter went on to become a habitual child molester—statistics suggest that he didn't. I think it was a case of a sexually confused teen who made a bad decision.

In nine out of ten sexual assaults, the victim knows the perpetrator. In roughly 35 to 40 percent of those cases, it's a relative. And if it's not a relative, it's Mom's new boyfriend (one of the more common victim-offender relationships) or, as in my case, a babysitter.

"The mythology of the dirty old man in the trench coat with the candy lurking around kids at a school yard is misplaced," says San Diego County Public Defender Marian Gaston. "The vast majority of sex offenders, they don't look like that...It's not this easily identifiable group of outsiders who can then be cast away. It's your sister's new boyfriend; it's your stepdad."

The term *sex offender* conjures the kind of monolithic image Gaston refers to—one that's reinforced by the news media and tough-on-crime politicians, despite evidence to the contrary.

Misperception and fear, rather than good empirical research, seem to be what drives sex-offender laws.

A case in point is a new law that takes effect this week in San Diego.

The "Child Protection" ordinance, passed unanimously by the City Council in March, is a spin-off of California's Jessica's Law, approved by voters in 2006. Among other things, Jessica's Law created mandatory sentences for sex offenders, requires that certain sex offenders be outfitted with Global Positioning System (GPS) devices for life, and expanded the list of what constitutes a sexual offense. Most controversial are the two-thousand-foot-radius "predator-free zones" the law established around schools and parks in which sex offenders who are paroled after November 7, 2006, are forbidden to live.

The law was named after Jessica Lunsford, a nine-year-old Florida girl who was abducted from her home, raped, and killed in 2005 by John Couey, a registered sex offender who lived about one hundred yards from the Lunsfords. Couey abducted Jessica by entering the home at night through an unlocked door.

Four unnamed plaintiffs—two from San Diego County—are challenging Jessica's Law before the state Supreme Court, arguing that the law's residency restrictions are too broad. None of the four's crimes involved children.

Despite the court challenge, San Diego went ahead and added more locations to the list of safe zones: city libraries, city parks, amusement parks (SeaWorld, the zoo), video arcades, licensed day-care facilities, and businesses that cater to children, like Chuck E. Cheese.

Additionally, the San Diego law creates "presence" restrictions that forbid registered sex offenders from being within three hundred feet of any of the above locations. While the city's enhanced residence restrictions apply only to people who commit a sexual offense after the law takes effect, the three-hundred-foot restriction applies to all registered sex offenders.

Sgt. Mark Sullivan, who supervises the San Diego Police Department's Sex Offender Registration Unit, said enforcement of the presence restriction would likely be complaint-driven.

"We used to get complaints from mothers that would take their kids to the park and say, 'There's a weird guy staring at my kids,' and they'd call the police, the police would show up [and] realize they're talking to a sex offender," Sullivan said, "but there was no law that would allow an officer to tell him to leave."

Now, under the new city law, the individual could be arrested, he said.

Unlike Jessica's Law, which has no defined punishment for anyone who violates the residence restriction (unless the person's on parole and, in that case, it's a parole violation), San Diego's ordinance makes it a misdemeanor criminal offense, punishable by up to six months in jail.

At the meeting where the City Council voted to implement the law, only one person spoke in opposition. Laura Arnold, a public defender, presented each council member with a ten-page memo that summarized what a number of studies have found: Restricting where a sex offender lives has no influence on whether or not he'll commit another crime. In fact, Arnold told the City Council, research has found that such restrictions can be counterproductive, pushing sex offenders into low-income communities and rural areas or, worse, onto the street.

In 2006, the California Coalition Against Sexual Assault, an umbrella group for eighty-four rape crisis centers and sexual-assault prevention programs, issued a strongly worded position statement opposing Jessica's Law: "Residency restrictions...don't make communities safer. Residency restrictions don't reduce recidivism, don't improve supervision of offenders, and ultimately do not protect children from sex offenders."

And, according to a study by the Minnesota Department of Corrections that looked specifically at repeat offenders, it really does come down to relationships and not geography: "What matters with respect to sexual recidivism is not residential proximity, but rather social or relationship proximity."

In 2006, the year before Jessica's Law went into effect, 2,000 sex offenders registered as transient with their local police agencies. According to recent numbers from the state, 3,140 sex offenders have registered as transient—a 63 percent increase in less than two years. In San Diego, roughly 200 of approximately 1,880 registered sex offenders have declared themselves homeless.

Sex offenders with permanent addresses are required to register annually or when they move, but transient registrants must check in with the police department every thirty days and provide officers with a general idea of where to find them, Sullivan said.

"They've made it very difficult for this population to find housing," said Steve Kubicek, supervisor of adult parole operations for San Diego County. "With the city, now you're adding [more locations]. It's almost as if they're purging the city of all registrants."

Transient registrants, Kubicek pointed out, are more likely to commit other crimes. "We may see an increase in drug use when they go on the streets," he said.

"Jessica's Law was passed hurriedly in an election year," he added. "And here we are in an election year.... I think [lawmakers'] intent was absolutely valid, but I think [the city law] was passed prior to evaluating the impact of the residency restriction."

In Iowa, where a similar two-thousand-foot rule has been in place since 2002, the Iowa County Prosecutors Association and more than three-dozen local governments have demanded that the state's legislature repeal the residence restriction because of the number of offenders who've gone underground. And in Miami-Dade County, a reporter for the weekly *Miami New Times* discovered roughly thirty men living under a freeway overpass, the only place they could legally reside from ten P.M. to six A.M. or risk violating probation or parole.

There are other consequences of residency restrictions. Laura Arnold recently had to find a way around the law to get a client into a drug treatment facility that was too close to a school. The client, a former prostitute, is a registered sex offender because she once said, "Show me your dick," to a vice cop. "Counseling" a person to expose himself is a sex crime.

Unlike most new laws the City Council enacts, this one got very little discussion; councilmembers talked in general terms about needing to protect children, and Councilmember Ben Hueso talked about how a similar National City ordinance was pushing sex offenders into his district and so the city needed to push back. There was no factual evidence presented to the public as to why the ordinance was needed.

Not only does the ordinance lack any clear reason for being, but also, as written, it contains wrong information, specifically a portion included in the "whereas" statements that lead off the document:

"According to a 1998 report by the U.S. Department of Justice, sex offenders are the least likely to be cured and the most likely to re-offend and prey on the most innocent members of our society, and more than two-thirds of victims of rape and sexual assault are under the age of 18, and sex offenders have a higher recidivism rate for their crimes than any other type of violent felon."

No such study exists. The information, rather, comes from a talk given by Florence Shapiro, a senator from Texas, at a 1998 conference organized by the Department of Justice. Shapiro was there to discuss Ashley's Law, her overhaul of Texas's sex-offender rules, prompted by the highly publicized death of Ashley Estell, a seven-year-old who, in 1993, was abducted from a playground and later found strangled. A man named Michael Blair, who'd helped search for the girl, was convicted and sentenced to death for her murder. Though an autopsy found no indication that Ashley had been sexually abused, Shapiro stuck with the story that the girl had been raped, and that's what she told the audience who gathered for the conference. Blair, twenty-three-years-old at the time of the trial and already a convicted child molester, damned himself by telling the jury that he saw nothing wrong with consensual sex with underage girls. (Blair's conviction is currently on appeal since repeated DNA tests of physical evidence suggest there were two men involved, neither of them Blair.)

Because Blair had served a shortened sentence for a child-molestation case, he became Shapiro's poster sex offender—if he'd remained in prison, she argued, Ashley would still be alive.

"Sex offenders are a very unique type of criminal," Shapiro told conference attendees. "I like to say they have three very unique characteristics: they are the least likely to be cured; they are the most likely to re-offend; and they prey on the most innocent members of our society."

Those words—attributed to a "U.S. Department of Justice study"—have made their way into various pieces of sex-offender legislation, like Jessica's Law and San Diego's new ordinance, even though the DOJ included a disclaimer along with the transcript of the conference, saying the contents "do not necessarily reflect the views and policies of the U.S. Department of Justice."

One part of the statement is true—more than two-thirds of victims of rape and sexual assault are under eighteen. But the rest of the information isn't accurate. A number of studies, including two by the Department of Justice (one released in 1997, another in 2003), have found that sex offenders have a much lower recidivism rate than any other type of criminal. According to the 1997 DOJ report, for which researchers tracked 272,111 parolees for three years, only 5.3 percent of the 9,691 sex offenders in the group were rearrested for another sex crime. As for the non-sex-offender cohort, 68 percent were rearrested. Other studies have found higher rates of recidivism among sex offenders—14 percent, on average, and as high as 26 percent—but still lower than for other criminals.

Parole's Kubicek said his own experience confirms what the studies have found. "It's very low for us for a new sex offense," he said.

As the state's Sex Offender Management Board put it, in its 219-page analysis of California's sex-offender laws, released in January, "Statements that sex offenders cannot be 'cured'—a concept generally accepted by experts in this field—have often been misinterpreted to mean that they will inevitably re-offend. In fact, the majority of sex offenders do not re-offend sexually over time."

Ultimately, though, debates about recidivism mean little when it comes to the population most affected by sexual assault. As Phyllis Shess, the deputy district attorney who heads the DA's sex-offender unit, pointed out, "You have to ask, is 1 percent [recidivism] acceptable? Is 10 percent acceptable? When you're talking about these kinds of issues, no, it isn't."

So what's the answer? Jessica's Law mandated that all "high-risk" felony sex offenders must wear a GPS device for life, so that their movement can be monitored by law enforcement. The California Department of Corrections and Rehabilitation began outfitting all newly paroled sex offenders—regardless of risk level—with some form of GPS device beginning last July.

In December, California was spending $21,000 a day on GPS monitoring, which comes out to $20 million a year. The state's Legislative Analyst's office estimated that within ten years, the cost for GPS monitoring could grow to $100 million annually and continue to increase. Right now local governments are expected to pick up the cost after a person completes parole, an idea that no municipality has yet embraced.

While some studies have found that GPS-monitored offenders have lower recidivism rates, pilot programs in San Diego and Tennessee found no significant difference between GPS-monitored sex offenders and those not on GPS. It's not necessarily going to stop someone who's dead-set on re-offending. "It's GPS, it's not real-time; you're not going to get the information until the following day."

If anything, it stops an offender from absconding, though the device can just as easily be cut off. The Tennessee Department of Corrections warned that GPS devices are a resource drain when used too broadly and shouldn't be used for lifelong monitoring. Successful rehabilitation requires that an offender be given a goal to work toward, the study found.

At a community forum on San Diego's Child Protection ordinance, Al Killen-Harvey, supervisor in the trauma counseling program at Rady Children's Hospital, questioned whether GPS devices were the best use of limited resources:

"We only have so much money, and that money's now gone to looking at these kinds of tracking devices. We've wiped out early prevention and education programs that we used to have fifteen and twenty years ago where we taught kids about healthy touch and bad touch and how to report it. We've wiped out funding for mental-health services for families that are economically distressed, which is a factor that may lead someone to cross a boundary that they wouldn't have crossed before.

"In the macro sense, yeah, we've missed the mark here, and we're allocating way too much money in an area where the bang for the buck is minimal compared to where the real risk level is," Killen-Harvey said.

His point on prevention is an important one. Eighty-seven percent of sex crimes committed each year are first-time offenses by people who aren't already known to the police. It's a statistic that turns public policy on its head—why put all the attention on the guys we already know about?

"There are agencies out there that have demonstrated that if you do a good public health, public awareness campaign, including a [hotline for] people who are afraid they might hurt a child…you can actually reduce the incidence of sexual assault in your community," said Marian Gaston, the public defender. "Why wouldn't we spend money on that? And instead, we're busy spending how many millions of dollars on GPS for people who are in their sixties and who are statistically just not going to do it again."

Then there's the issue of treatment. The public's perception is that treatment doesn't work—a sex offender is a sex offender for life. But not everyone who molests a child fits the clinical definition of a pedophile, for one thing—sometimes other self-destructive factors drive behavior, like drug addiction. Recent studies have shown that, for repeat offenders, therapy does, in fact, lead to lower recidivism rates. California, however, is one of the few states that don't offer in-custody treatment; only once a person's released from custody is treatment mandated. It's puzzling, given that Jessica's Law is putting people behind bars longer.

The California Department of Corrections and Rehabilitation has plans to build a new locked treatment facility for sex offenders, but, as the state's Sex Offender Management Board pointed out in its January report, nothing's moved beyond the planning stage.

Anyone who falls into the category of "sexually violent predator," based on a prerelease assessment, is turned over to one of two state mental hospitals, rather than paroled, where the individual goes through a multiphase treatment program, is reassessed and then, if he's found by a judge to be stable enough, released back into the community.

Once someone's off probation or parole, treatment ends and it's rare that those who need it will seek it voluntarily, said Shess, the deputy district attorney.

"We did an experiment through the [county's] Sexual Offender Management Council, offering resources to people who felt like stresses—whatever it was in their life that might be putting them in a situation where they might re-offend—and no one took advantage of it. The counseling wasn't free, but it would have been low cost," Shess said. And, even then, the county would have made arrangements for someone who couldn't afford to pay. "We didn't even get that far. Nobody called to say, 'Hey I'm a prior offender, I'm feeling like I might need help'—no one."

Around 90 percent of sex offenders aren't under state or county supervision, Kubicek noted. "The 10 percent that are on parole are receiving the best supervision available," he said. "My concern is, how do we enforce the 90 percent who are receiving no supervision, who are just registering?"

One might assume that when a sex offender goes in to register with the police each year (or, each month if he's a transient), there might be a brief talk with a counselor or some other kind of assessment that happens. But, aside from an initial assessment when an individual first registers, there's not much follow-up. The city of San Diego has only five officers dedicated to the sexual-assault unit (which includes sex-offender management): one sergeant (Mark Sullivan), two detectives and two code-compliance officers who staff the office where more than one hundred people go to register each week.

What if, rather than putting restrictions on where a sex offender can live and move about town—strategies whose effectiveness isn't supported by evidence—the City Council pledged to fund a risk-assessment counselor for the police department? Sure, money's short, but it's hard to argue when it comes to protecting kids. Hire an intake counselor or set up a hotline that someone like my mom could call to find out how to respond when her kid says the baby-sitter's asking her to do things she doesn't understand.

Another thing to think about: it's difficult to turn in a friend or relative when you know that, unlike any other crime, this is one that will follow the person around for the rest of his life. Would my mom have turned the guy over to police if it meant a lifetime of public scrutiny and, in essence, banishment?

Probably not.

War Games: No WMDs but Military
Police Find "Dangerous" Dildos in Iraq

Tom Johansmeyer

In the middle of the night on July 5, 2007, U.S. Air Force Military Police cleared the 402nd Field Support Brigade's barracks. When the dust settled, the MPs had walked away with armfuls of contraband taken from the soldiers and civilian contractors stationed at Camp Anaconda in Iraq. The illicit fare removed from the facility included liquor, adult videos, and novelty items—all prohibited under U.S. Army Central Command's (CENTCOM's) General Order 1a (GO-1a).

For civilian contractors, the punishment for possession of contraband is the immediate loss of employment; military personnel can be prosecuted either judicially or nonjudicially under the Uniform Code of Military Justice (UCMJ).

Through the course of the search, MPs discovered dildos owned by two civilian contractors and confiscated them under the assumption that they were contraband. Immediately, the women feared that they would lose their jobs, but the MPs later were advised by legal authorities that dildos are not considered pornography—and that the women should be permitted to keep their jobs.

GO-1a explicitly forbids the possession of pornographic materials in Iraq, but it does not define clearly what is prohibited, making anything but the most monastic lifestyle a daily risk of unemployment or other penalties. The ambiguity inherent in GO-1a makes attempts at enforcement perfectly comical to all except those personally affected.

The Military's Rules on Porn

GO-1a, issued by General Tommy Franks on December 19, 2000, explicitly prohibits the possession or use of privately owned firearms and explosives, entry into a mosque except as directed by military authorities, making or consuming alcohol, drugs, and drug paraphernalia, gambling, currency exchange, and "proselytizing."

The rationale for GO-1a, according to the order itself, is to "preserv[e] U.S./host nation relations and combined operations of U.S. and friendly forces." This need arises from the fact that "[c]urrent operations and deployments place United States Armed Forces into…countries where local laws and customs prohibit or restrict certain activities which are generally permissible in western societies."

Fifth on the list of prohibited activities is the "[i]ntroduction, possession, transfer, sale, creation, or display of any pornographic or sexually explicit photograph, videotapes, movie, drawing, book, magazine, or similar representations." GO-1a continues, "The prohibitions contained in this paragraph shall not apply to AFRTS [Armed Forces Radio and Television Services] broadcasts and commercial videotapes distributed and/or displayed through AAFES [Army and Air Force Exchange Services] or MWR [Military Welfare and Recreation] outlets located within CENTCOM AOR [Area of Responsibility]."

What does this clumsily worded regulation mean? Anybody under the responsibility of CENTCOM, including both military and civilian personnel, cannot have any sexually explicit material unless it is delivered via military-approved broadcast or retail outlets. A magazine with bare breasts is not contraband if it is sold by AAFES (which manages the PX and BX stores on military installations), and a film with sexual themes is not obscene if it is screened for troops in a MWR center. Computers in MWR centers even allow the use of social networking websites such as MySpace, though this (and other social networking websites) is not permitted outside the MWR context.

Riddled with exceptions in the way it was crafted and enforced, GO-1a lacks a straightforward definition of "pornographic or sexually explicit." While oral, vaginal, or anal penetration, for example, usually signal pornography, anything else relies on Justice Potter Stewart's 1964 standard: "I know it when I see it." Unfortunately, General Tommy Franks was not available to supervise every inspection in Iraq personally. An unusually stringent or lax commander can create a different culture under GO-1a, with different standards for "sexually explicit."

At a commander's discretion, the term "sexually explicit" could be used to outlaw full or partial nudity, clothed models in suggestive poses, or mainstream books that contain nude sketches. As written, GO-1a would apply only to adult novelty items that resemble (i.e., are "similar representations" of) banned body parts that would violate GO-1a. A smooth, plain plastic vibrator thus would probably pass the test while a textured item resembling a penis would not.

GO-1a characterizes online adult entertainment material as obscene and therefore prohibited, and military and civilian contractor

Internet use is carefully controlled. Soldiers and civilians serving in Iraq are not permitted to visit websites that could be construed as having offensive material, including the benign photography enthusiast website Photo.net. Since Photo.net has a section about photographing art nudes, the military has deemed it off limits.

Photography and porn devotees can sidestep government Internet filters, but it is expensive, according to Brian Sayler. Sayler spent nearly two years in Iraq as a civilian contractor with KBR and ITT before losing his job for possessing adult films that were found during the July 5th inspection. Sayler explains that individuals can secure personal Internet connections for their rooms using satellite equipment that can cost up to three thousand dollars. After installation, the service requires an ongoing fee that can reach one hundred and fifty dollars a month.

With this personal Internet service, one can access anything on the Web, as military filters are not applied, but GO-1a still governs the use of these Internet connections. The military simply lacks the means to physically restrict access, but the policy remains in effect. The semblance of privacy afforded by private Internet connections can dissipate when computer problems need to be resolved (e.g., from viruses).

"The IT [information technology] guys have to repair computers loaded with porn all the time," he explains. "They even get computers from Lieutenant Colonels that are full of porn. Usually, they just delete it or tell the guy not to go to porn sites anymore," taking no further action. Rank, it seems, has its privileges. The context in which porn is discovered and one's standing in the military hierarchy can mean the difference between a polite request not to violate GO-1a and the decimation of a career.

The absence of clear guidance as to what constitutes contraband coupled with a sometimes permissive attitude and ungoverned Internet access contributed to the debacle with the 402nd Field Support Brigade, but the mistake was avoidable. Had Command Sergeant Major Vela, who personally initiated the inspection by contacting the MPs and issuing the order, simply documented the scope and nature of the inspection, the likelihood of error—and subsequent embarrassment—would have been reduced substantially.

Health and Welfare Inspections—A Time-Honored Tradition

The military thrives on order and accountability. The absence of discipline degrades the capabilities of the fighting force. If a military commander devises or implements any policy for the purposes of maintaining discipline, it is generally for a reason. In regard to contraband, the primary means of maintaining such discipline is the "health and welfare inspection."

An invasive process, these inspections occur unannounced in the middle of the night. Surprise prevents those being inspected from concealing or disposing of contraband. The housing facility being examined is cleared of all inhabitants, and each resident is escorted back into the barracks as his or her room is being inspected, a measure intended to ensure that those conducting the inspection do not steal or damage an individual's permissible property. Soldiers and civilian contractors must wait outside until their turns arise, then watch as bags, bureaus, and wall lockers are ransacked and prohibited personal belongings removed.

The health and welfare inspection that CSM Vela ordered for July 5, 2007 generally followed this pattern, though the administrative aspects of his inspection differed substantially from the norm.

Contrary to the manner in which the 402nd Field Support Brigade conducted its health and welfare inspection, the process is not a blank check for search and seizure. In most cases, a memorandum for record is written in advance, specifying the scope of the search. This measure, suggested by the army's Judge Advocate General Corp (JAG), intended to prove that an inspection is not a subterfuge for illegal search.

JAG suggests that the memorandum state the date and time of the inspection, locations to be inspected (e.g. rooms or facilities), and areas within rooms to be searched. CSM Vela did not write a memorandum for record to support the July 5, 2007 health and welfare inspection at Camp Anaconda. Instead, he simply called the MPs and initiated the inspection.

During most health and welfare inspections, the searches of individual rooms are conducted in the presence of the room's resident(s); the MPs following CSM Vela's direction did not observe this standard. Instead, those inspected had to wait outside the building, unable to ensure that personal property was not damaged or confiscated unnecessarily. As a result, the dildo affair could have been avoided, as well as the confiscation of a laptop computer (belonging to Sayler).

Though his laptop was returned prior to his removal from Camp Anaconda, Sayler lost a number of videos in the search that were autographed and given to him by adult film performer Cassidey. Her gesture, she made clear to him at a public appearance in April 2007, was a show of support for those serving in Iraq. When told of the July 5th inspection, she wrote, *I am upset that such things can be a reason for [a civilian contractor's] getting fired. We send our boys off to fight in a war that is not even ours, and [they] get fired...for that shit?*

And then there is the issue of the dildos.

The MPs were not sufficiently trained as to the definitions of pornography and sexually explicit material, and they were unaware that adult novelty items were not banned under GO-1a. While the military can dismiss the seizure of personal property as a mistake, absolving the MPs involved in the search of error, a memorandum for record could have prevented mistakes and embarrassment. Had CSM provided some guidance via a memorandum for record, the dildos might have been discovered, but they would have remained where they were found. Sayler's laptop (containing personal and financial records) would not have been withheld.

Captain William Englebert, Camp Anaconda's Provost (the MPs' "police chief"), indicated privately to Sayler that "mistakes were made," which he emphasized occurred before he became Provost. In addition to taking permitted personal items, such as the laptop and dildos, the leaders of the 402nd Field Support Brigade (CSM Vela and his commander, Colonel Sorenson) allowed the names of the affected women to be leaked, making dignity the cost of a paycheck. CSM Vela did not respond to email requests for comment.

Porn Still Supports the Troops

Since the start of the war, the adult entertainment community has been quite vocal in its support of the troops, if not the war itself. Industry executives and performers alike have genuine feelings of compassion for those who risk their lives every day in combat theaters around the world. Carmen Luvana asks, "What is the harm in soldiers' wanting to get off for a minute to get rid of all the stress they have...as long as they are not doing it in front of anybody?"

In 1993, for example, Army Rangers in Somalia had copious access to such outlets, a fact that is well documented in Mark Bowden's *Black Hawk Down*. At some point in the seven years that followed, the military reversed course. While the policy has changed, much remains the same. Soldiers face hostile fire in a foreign country. The "host nation" in each case had cultural biases against pornography. This time, though, society's selfless are not allowed even the most primal of comforts.

The "about face" executed since 1993 indicates a change in tolerance, but the industry remains unwavering in its support for those who defend freedom. The First Amendment rights on which the industry relies make the military's role in defending freedom tangible, more real than it is to critics of adult entertainment. Without the free society that our military is sworn to defend, the porn industry would cease to exist, and we are left thinking, as starlet Hannah Harper does, that "it is a shame that the freedoms the soldiers cannot enjoy are the freedoms they are fighting and dying for."

In Defense of Casual Sex
Tracy Clark-Flory

Twenty-something Anna Broadway has known many men—so many, in fact, that she's given them each an easy nickname, like Singapore Fling, Sugar Daddy, Internet Date, and Married Man. She's met them on Craigslist, through online dating sites, and at singles bars. Broadway sounds a lot like your average member of the "hookup" generation, save for one detail: none of these men have made it into her bed. That's because, as Broadway writes in her memoir, *Sexless in the City,* she's saving herself for marriage.

Broadway's G-rated memoir is just one of a slew of books about chastity released in time to make everyone's list of hot summer reads...for those planning a vacation in the Arctic Circle. The onslaught started in the spring with *Sex and the Soul: Juggling Sexuality, Spirituality, Romance, and Religion on America's College Campuses,* which reports that all but marriage-minded evangelical students are sleeping around—and attending Pimps 'n' Hos parties—in hopes of meeting that special someone. Next came *The Purity Code,* a book for Christian teens detailing "God's plan for sex and your body." The catalog climaxed with the August 1 release of *Hooked: New Science on How Casual Sex Is Affecting Our Children.* (Hint: cataclysmically.)

These books are just the latest result of the mounting abstinence movement, which, despite its religious roots, has recast its attack on "hookup" culture as secular, even feminist. The term "hooking up"—meaning anything from kissing to casual sex—can be traced back to the early '80s, but only within the past few years did the hand-wringing really begin. Former *Washington Post* reporter Laura Sessions Stepp spent years detailing so-called collegiate mating rituals—often lamenting a tendency among young women toward boozed-up hookups instead of cross-legged gatekeeping—which culminated in last year's retro revitalization, *Unhooked: How Young Women Pursue Sex, Delay Love, and Lose at Both.*

The abstinence movement has been successful in securing federal funding for abstinence-only programs—to the tune of eight hundred million[1] over the past eight years—but the spectacle of father-daughter purity balls, chastity rings, and virginity pledges has failed to make abstinence appear even marginally cool to the mainstream. More recently, activists have begun borrowing from the feminist arsenal—using words like "empowerment" and "respect"—in their assault on uncommitted sex. These books add to a loud cautionary chorus: Young women are hooking up and tuning out emotionally. And, increasingly, young women are being told they are either respecting or exploiting themselves; they're either with the *Girls Gone Wild,* sex blogger set or with the iron-belted and chaste. A few months back, a *New York Times Magazine* piece about chastity on Ivy League campuses relied on this false binary: it pitted a prim Harvard abstinence advocate against a campus sex blogger (who recently posted a photo of her face covered in splooge).

Choose a side? No thanks. I'm a twenty-four-year-old member of the hookup generation—I've had roughly three times as many hookups as relationships—and, like innumerable twentysomethings before me, I've found that casual sex can be healthy and normal and lead to better adult relationships. I don't exactly advocate picking up guys at frat parties and screwing atop the keg as the path to marital bliss. It's just that hookup culture is not the radical extreme it is so frequently mischaracterized as in the media. There is sloppy stranger sex among people my age, sure, but sometimes hooking up is regular sex with a casual acquaintance; sometimes it's innocent making out or casually dating or cuddling, and, oftentimes it involves just one person at a time. In a sense it's all very old-fashioned—there's just a lot more unattached sex involved.

Like most twentysomethings, I've had online pornography and unregulated chatrooms at my fingertips since I hit puberty. But I also grew up during the Girl/Grrrl Power explosion, which taught me to demand respect, and play handball (and, later, hardball) with the boys. And it taught me that I didn't need to cake myself in makeup or teeter along in foot-disfiguring heels—unless, of course, I wanted to.

From the very start, my love life has embodied that seeming paradox. I lost my virginity at sixteen with my first love and best friend; it was all champagne and roses. It was also as-porn-ational sex: I enthusiastically guided us into nearly every position I'd long marveled at online. At one point, midcoital, I actually pinched my chin and asked aloud, "What positions are left?" Afterward, he observed: "That wasn't what I'd imagined, exactly." He had imagined: 1) the missionary position and 2) ceremonial crying.

I didn't do much hooking up in college; I went to a single-sex school. But after I closed the gates to that cosseted women's school—and all of its unsexy talk about misogyny and *the patriarchy*—I opened those other, um, metaphorical gates of mine. Okay, screw the modesty: my legs, I opened my legs. That's not to say I had a host of one-night stands—I've never had a one-night stand, only several-nights stands. But I went through a dressing room phase of trying on different men to see how they fit. (This one makes my control-freak quotient look big but has a slimming effect on my ego.) Like Anna Broadway, I can easily and embarrassingly categorize these men: Lonely Lawyer, Sociopathic Spaniard, Testosterone-Poisoned Pilot, and Bellicose Bartender, for starters. Together, they're like the Village People for straight women. During this time, I told my friend Sarah and her boyfriend about the latest person I was seeing. "Which one?" he asked, smirking. I laughed, but I wondered: *Shit, am I that girl?*

For a while, I was. First, there was the cartoonist. The first night we hooked up, he took me back to his house and played guitar, sang every song he'd ever written, and juggled his collection of vitamin pill bottles.

Then there was the lawyer. We would have passionate, hours-long debates, as though we were opposing counsels in court; the first of such debates ended with him throwing up his hands and announcing, "Congratulations, you've worn out a professional litigator." He owned his own three-story house with a panorama of the Bay Area, drove an SUV—with a shiny hood ornament that made me cringe—and wanted to sweep me off my feet, rescue me from my one-room apartment, as well as the dishes piled up in (and under) my sink, and my bipolar upstairs neighbor whose monologues are the constant soundtrack to my home life. I told him, "No thanks," and moved along.

Then there was the pilot, whom I would see whenever his flight schedule brought him into town. I'd stay the night at his utilitarian airport hotel, order room service, watch planes take off right outside our window, and talk about sexy things like black boxes, plane crashes, and thunderstorms. He was cartoonishly masculine and he made me feel stereotypically feminine, which I am not; it made me constantly want to challenge him to an arm-wrestling match. It was amorous antagonism.

As far as I can tell, these choices don't form a pattern, other than a refusal to really choose. I was like a college freshman filling out the Career Center's job placement questionnaire, making an enthusiastic check mark next to every box; except, in my case, I was checking off men. Most of them were great; others led me on and made me cry. In a few cases, I felt used, but other times I felt like a user. There were some I wanted to date but who wanted to keep things casual, and vice versa.

There's nothing unusual about my experience. The *New York Times* recently ran a "Modern Love" essay by Marguerite Fields, a college junior, about her search for a boy willing to commit. Like me, and like Broadway, she has worked her way through a number of men and says, "I think what I have been seeking in some form from all of these men is permanence." Near the end of her essay, she ends a third date by asking the guy when she'll see him next. "That's a loaded question," he says, offering a meandering explanation: "He said he had just gotten out of a long relationship, and now he was single and didn't really know how this whole dating thing works, but he was seeing a lot of other people, and he liked me."

I've heard that speech before; I've given that speech before. It shouldn't be mistaken as a symptom of a generation unable to commit; it's simply what you tell someone when you realize that you don't like him or her all that much. For all the anxiety about "hookup culture" the truth is that for many people older than twenty, "hookup culture" will sound remarkably like, well, "college." Indeed, students shifted from dating to what was essentially hooking up during a wild time—perhaps you've heard of it—called the '70s.

But, as the median age of marriage continues to climb, young women are spending a lot more time romantically vetting—and being vetted. It isn't just that hooking up is becoming a common preamble to dating, either—living in sin is increasingly a prelude to marriage. Hopefully, by taking several test-drives before buying, we'll be happier with our final investment.

Of course, there are also very real hazards to hookup culture: namely, rising rates of unplanned pregnancies among young women and sky-high STD rates. It's safe to say many don't take the latter very seriously: Moe Tkacik, a blogger for Gawker Media's feminist blog, Jezebel, recently stirred the pot by writing that condomless sex "feels awesome" because she has "only really engaged in bareback sex with the types of dudes…whose diseases I don't particularly fear, because the worst thing I can think of about most of them is the ensuing lifetime of awkward conversations." (And, occasionally, sexual empowerment is overplayed to the point of farce, in the case of a recent incident in which Moe and fellow blogger Tracie Egan shrugged off the seriousness of rape.)

But much of the finger-wagging over hooking up neglects those very reasonable concerns. For example, abstinence advocates are fond of the saying: "There is no condom for the heart." But heartbreak isn't always sexually transmitted. In the *New York Times Magazine* piece on chastity, prominent Harvard activist Janie Fredell lamented the hurt she'd seen women go through in their pursuit of relationships via hooking up—as though abstaining from sex would have saved them a broken heart. If only.

I learned something from all of the men I dated. Sexually, I learned plenty about what turns me on. More important, by spending time in uncommitted relationships, what I wanted in a committed relationship became clearer—and it wasn't amorous antagonism but a partnership that didn't trigger self-protectiveness.

I also discovered that a lot of young men are scared shitless—of women, themselves, and their future; that, contrary to our cultural imaginings, they are just as desperate to figure things out as young women. I found that a lot of the pains in the relationships of us twentysomethings can be blamed on cultural prescriptions for masculinity. Yes, there is the stud/slut double standard—but there's also an expectation that men, unlike women, will not seek safe harbor in a relationship. No, they are supposed to bravely sail their ships beyond the singing sirens and silted waters of their quarter life until they miraculously hit land in the Real Adult World.

As Kathy Dobie wrote in reviewing Stepp's *Unhooked:* "We learn less about intimacy in our youthful sex lives than we do about humanity...Perhaps, this generation, by making sex less precious, less a commodity, will succeed in putting simple humanity back into sex." Indeed, and perhaps young women are putting feminist ideals of equality into sex by refusing shame and claiming the traditionally male side of the stud/slut double standard. Also, the idea that a woman has to test a man by withholding sex—as many abstinence advocates actually argue—relies on a paradigm of inequality in which women are forced to rely on such desperate power plays. It isn't that feminism has taught women to have sex like men, as the argument commonly goes, but that withholding sex isn't women's sole superpower; coitus isn't women's kryptonite.

With that in mind, I put my academic and career achievements ahead of romantic relationships, and allowed myself plenty of uncommitted entertainment along the way.

Like Broadway, I happily stayed single until I found someone who seemed truly worth the commitment; unlike Broadway, I wasn't abstinent. These *can* be different paths ultimately converging on the same plateau of partnership. By the same token, though, you can chastely date more men than you can count—or sleep with every man who offers you a drink—and not learn a damn thing about how to find a healthy relationship. We feminists do, indeed, love words like *empowerment* and *respect,* but there's one we like even more: *choice.* The problem is that, too often, the abstinence movement prescribes a particular path, rather than encouraging young women to blaze their own trail.

A year ago, I decided to take a brief hookup hiatus and then, unexpectedly, met a man who is emotionally available and comfortably, not defensively, masculine—I've never felt the need to challenge him to an arm-wrestling match. We're in a relationship now and he has become my best friend. He openly calls himself a feminist and, smilingly, describes our relationship as "respect run amok."

Oh, and we had sex the first night we met.

NOTES:

1. http://www.nastad.org/Docs/Public/Resource/200759/_Abstinence Fact Sheet.pdf

Soulgasm
Dagmar Herzog

Antimasturbation and abstinence guidance is not the only graphically detailed evangelical advice out there. Obsessing over orgasms has also long been an essential ingredient of the evangelical sex advice business. For at least a quarter-century, evangelical sex advice-givers have recognized that every man and woman wants bigger and better orgasms. They know this is as true for their flock as it is for the average forsaken nonbeliever. And so they have turned their attention to techniques for intensifying climax.

God wants His devoted followers to have boundary-dissolving ecstasy each and every time. There is no need to feel unfulfilled and frustrated after sex with a spouse. Evangelicals deserve the very best in sex, and so evangelical experts offer the happy news that holy sex means orgasmic sex. Dozens upon dozens of evangelical publications rehearse the basic facts of life. *Cosmo* meets the Bible.

Evangelicals Linda Dillow and Lorraine Pintus provide one of the most popular guides for Christian women and their orgasmic lives: *Intimate Issues* (published, like the "Every Man" series, by WaterBrook Press, an evangelical Christian publishing house based in Colorado Springs, Colorado, and a division of Random House). Coining the term "soulgasm" as the desired result of sex with your husband—incredible orgasms *plus* intense emotional connection with your husband *plus* God's spiritual presence—Dillow and Pintus describe the experience variously: "Waves of pleasure flow over me; it feels like sliding down a mountain waterfall." Or: "It's like having a million tiny pleasure balloons explode inside of me all at once."

Orgasm equity is key to the Dillow and Pintus vision. They are unapologetic in their insistence that Christian women make their own pleasure a priority. They recommend that women "EXERCISE YOUR LOVE MUSCLE. Your PC muscle (pubococcygeal) is your love muscle." They describe the "SIX SECRETS OF HIGHLY ORGASMIC WIVES," which include not only "grab your Nikes" (because a well-exercised woman is also a pleasure-primed one) but also "educate yourself" about your own body. Above all, they urge women to "let yourself feel":

> As Christians, we often think that focusing on ourselves is wrong, that we should concentrate on giving, not receiving. But in order to move toward physical orgasm, we must give ourself [*sic*] permission to dwell on our physical responses and emotional feelings…It is not selfish…There is a fascinating paradox as your selfish inward journey to orgasm and intense personal excitement become a mutual experience and a marvelous turn-on for your mate.

Dillow and Pintus are enormously reassuring in their sensible advice that every woman—like every couple—is unique, and that "there is no 'right way' to make love." So they also stress that while clitoral pleasuring may be the key to orgasm for the majority of women, some women experience their orgasms as centered in the vagina. And they point out that simultaneous orgasm is not a necessary aim; it is perfectly fine for women to come first. Indeed, "some couples find that intercourse is more pleasurable for the women [*sic*] if she has already reached a climax as her genitals are lubricated and engorged."

And they go out of their way as well to answer the query "Is intercourse the only 'proper' way to have sex?" by asserting that, no, "intercourse is not the *only* 'proper' way to have sex," because "God grants us enormous liberty" and "we are free to enjoy sexual variety." They recommend to their female readers the following prayer: *"Lord, keep me growing as a godly and sensuous woman. Keep me from worrying about what is normal and let me dwell on what is a successful sexual encounter for me and my husband."* If all goes well, and all lessons are practiced and learned, Dillow and Pintus assure their female readers that this story of "Bethany" might someday be their own story:

> It had never occurred to me that I could come more than once. Then I read that this sometimes happened to women as they grew in giving in to their sexuality and in their trust of their husbands. I think reading about it opened the door—and the next time we were making love I experienced wave after wave of pleasure. As he entered me, I built up to another orgasm. It wasn't something I tried to make happen, but it was glorious, and my husband felt like "Superman lover."

Testimonials like these are another crucial component of the evangelical sex industry: true tales from real people who find orgasmic bliss through prayer and devotion—and by flexing their love muscles.

When evangelicals talk about sex, they inhabit a world of religious references that make sense to them. A typical recommendation is: "Try this simple act of foreplay: Pray with her." Nor would eyebrows be raised by the answer to the question *"How Do I Shift into Sexual Gear?"*: "1. Memorize the first portion of Romans 12:2: Do not be conformed to this world, but be transformed by the renewing of your mind."

Yet, as the experts suggest over and over again, evangelicals struggle with anxiety about what they are permitted to do with one another. As marriage therapists and clergy counselors Louis and Melissa McBurney put it in their essay, "Christian Sex Rules: A Guide to What's Allowed in the Bedroom," they receive "many, many questions from Christian couples who want to know what is and what is not okay to do sexually." Or as Dillow and Pintus note, "Many women we talk with want to be reassured that their sex life is normal." Yet "normal" is not always an easy thing to define, even for the true believer. (And certainly doing so has not gotten any easier in the midst of new pressures and challenges wrought by sexual psychopharmacology and Internet pornography.)

There is no consensus among the faithful as to what constitutes good clean sexual fun. To be told that 1 Corinthians 7:1-5 reveals that "the Bible clearly promotes the value of regular sexual release" is considered pertinent, if perhaps ambivalently received, information. Being told that the Song of Solomon celebrates oral pleasuring for men and women can be a huge relief for some. A few Christian advice-writers reject the idea that the Song of Solomon offers guidelines for sexual practice, yet many argue otherwise. The LaHayes in their 1976 classic were among the first to suggest that the Song of Solomon, especially verses 2:6 and 8:3, might be translated into tips for genital pleasuring. And Joseph Dillow (Linda's husband) dedicated an entire book to the naughtiness of *Solomon on Sex* in 1982.

In his book, Dillow offers a close reading of Song of Solomon 4:5: "They two breasts are like two young roes that are twins, which feed among the lilies," and then riffs on Solomon's interest in "his wife's breasts": "They are very curvaceous like the lily. Their beauty creates within his heart a desire to reach out and fondle them as one would a gazelle feeding by a brook. The notion of frolicksomeness suggests sexual playfulness." And "the female genitals are referred to in 5:1 as a 'garden' and in 4:13 as 'shoots.' In both passages, myrrh and frankincense are described as characteristic scents of her 'garden.'"

Other evangelicals have made similar enthusiastic claims that the Song of Solomon is a detailed account of the sexual foreplay and "total body involvement" enjoyed between King Solomon and his beloved, and that the Song of Solomon describes "passionate lovemaking" and "sexual climax—higher and higher," "ecstasy," "orgasm," and "sexual oneness." It all gets pretty steamy in the retelling. As one writer summarized the accumulated wisdom in 2000, "The Song of Solomon…is one of the best textbooks for sexual instruction ever printed."

Another writer assures his male readers: "If you're a husband who wants to be a consummate lover to your wife, learn from Solomon. Once you start understanding the idioms of Solomon's day, you'll see that he knew exactly how to bring his wife to peaks of sexual ecstasy. Do what he did, and your wife will respond as passionately as his." Never mind that a few pages earlier, the same author concedes that "rich and powerful men like King David and King Solomon had not only a multitude of wives but concubines, as well, to sate their need for status and sexual gratification."

Not that Song of Solomon is the final word on sexual dos and don'ts. There are a host of thorny issues that continue to challenge evangelical sex writers as they confront what should be deemed proper or improper behavior in bed. For instance, there is the not-inconsequential matter of oral sex. In this regard, Tim Alan Gardner's *Sacred Sex: A Spiritual Celebration of Oneness in Marriage* stands firmly with the naysayers. Gardner informs the faithful that

> If you receive your sexual information primarily from the magazine rack at the grocery checkout lane, you'll believe things like "every man loves getting oral sex and every woman loves giving it." In reality, however, studies show that this is not true. A majority of women do not like giving or receiving oral sex, and most men don't find it the most enjoyable way to engage sexually. The reason everybody is talking about it is simply because everyone is talking about it.

Evangelicals cannot agree about the righteousness of oral sex. Marriage and sex advice author Karin Brown acknowledges that there is considerable unease among Christians over the activity of oral sex, and she admits that often either the man or the woman does not particularly enjoy it or feels forced into it by their partner. She notes that "so many marriages seem to be plagued with disagreement regarding it." Yet Brown says she favors the activity, although she is careful to advise that it be used solely for foreplay and not as a substitute for intercourse.

There are also sex toys to puzzle over. Take vibrators. This time Karin Brown heads up the opposition: "I personally see no need for them when we have hands, lips, and other great body parts to successfully heighten our intimate sexual encounters." But Dillow and Pintus demur. They ask that the faithful apply the following test: "To find out if the use of a vibrator is right or wrong, let's apply the three questions. Is the use of a vibrator prohibited by Scripture? Is a vibrator beneficial to lovemaking? Does the use of a vibrator involve anyone else?" Since scripture does not offer commentary on vibrators—rendering it acceptable from a scriptural perspective—Dillow and Pintus move rapidly to questions two and three. On this basis they conclude: "So if a vibrator enhances a couple's lovemaking and is used exclusively for the couple's private enjoyment, then it is permitted."

This is the commonsensical view adopted by a number of evangelical writers. Examine scripture and if there is nothing to prohibit a specific activity there, then it ought to be permitted. On this score, evangelicals Melissa McBurney and Louis McBurney emerge as virtual sex libertarians. The McBurneys have concluded, with regard to "oral sex, rear-entry vaginal penetration…and mutual masturbation," that since "we find no scriptural injunction against any of these," they are all just fine.

Evangelical authors have given thumbs-up to all sorts of activities one might not immediately assume to be appropriate evangelical behavior. Sexy lingerie? This has been interpreted as a definite plus, again with reference to the Song of Solomon. Anal sex? Hard to imagine? On the contrary, while some evangelicals deem anal sex unhealthy, there is the loving couple Reverend Charles Shedd and his wife Martha, who have testified that their own sexual experiments have included anal sex, and they have publicly pronounced it enjoyable indeed. So too do the Reverends Paula and Lori Byerly of the online site The Marriage Bed, which is officially antiporn, feel comfortable recommending both oral and anal sex, as well as a wife masturbating while her husband gets to watch. For the Byerlys, in marriage you can do just about anything. Typical upbeat advice includes enthusiastic endorsement of the "come-hither" move, in which the husband uses his fingers to stimulate his wife's G-spot—"We think the G-spot should be seen as one more way God gave us to share in the pleasure of sex"—as well as the seemingly neutral observation that just because the Bible says homosexual sex (as well as, they note, homosexual kissing) is wrong does not in any way prove that anal sex is wrong. They also note that spanking can be "arousing" and that bondage can be "very arousing."

Recently, evangelicals have also begun increasingly to recommend that couples engage in occasional quickies. As Tim Alan Gardner states in *Sacred Sex:*

> I like to think of healthy marital sexual encounters in three categories....The first grouping is Fast-Food Sex. This primarily includes "quickies" and those spur-of-the-moment rendezvouses that take place without a lot of planning. Frequently, only the husband will have an orgasm (though not always). Fast food is fine, on occasion, but too much of it will leave one or both of you lacking passion and feeling taken for granted just as too many triple cheeseburgers will leave you—well, let's just say, not healthy.

Gardner's two other recipes for a healthy marriage are Informal Dining and Five-Star Dining.

Gardner is far from alone. Dillow and Pintus also endorse the quickie, by which "we are talking about the act of sex taking around three to five minutes." The quickie, these women assure their presumably female readers, is absolutely "okay with God."

How do we explain the evangelical advocacy of the quickie? First, there is the worry that with women's growing equality in the world and growing concern with enhancing women's orgasm equity, men don't seem to feel terribly special anymore. Second, there is the much-discussed phenomenon that the supersaturation of the visual landscape with sexualized images—from Internet porn in the home to racy fashions on the street—has been accompanied by a perceived plummet in heterosexual desire. Viewed in this double context, the evangelicals' obsession with male ego-boosting and the novel attacks against masturbation and fantasy make more sense. And this is also the context in which the quickie—fine for the man, less so (usually) for the woman—should be understood.

The extent to which evangelicals embrace their version of the sexual revolution and the feminist movement is striking. As Shannon Ethridge writes: "I'm thrilled that the women's liberation movement brought us freedom to vote, get an education, and find satisfaction in careers." And Stephen Arterburn clearly understands the necessity for husbands serving their wives, especially the many who work outside the home, by cooking, cleaning, doing the dishes, sharing child care responsibilities, and so forth. These are the legacies of women's liberation that the evangelical movement supports 100 percent.

Yet evangelical writers on sex unapologetically contradict themselves. On the one hand, they admonish men that they never have a "biblical right" to demand sexual submission from their wives. They assure wives that they need never engage in any sexual practice they find degrading or unpleasant. In fact, they urgently remind wives that to accept the biblical injunction to wifely "submission" does not mean mindlessly doing whatever their husbands tell them to do.

On the other hand, the authors of the "Every Man" series, for instance, also recommend that wives be sexually available to their husbands at all times. Women should meet their men's needs with tenderness and compassion—and, if need be, with those quickies. Even Shannon Ethridge encourages wives to keep their legs shaved and their vaginas douched at all times. Just in case.

Despite their seeming support for women's equality at home and in the workplace, moreover, evangelical authors spend a great deal of time repeating what they call "a foundational truth:

God created men and women to be different."

That women don't want sex as often as men is a regular feature in the archives of Christian sex literature. Dr. Neil T. Anderson, founder and president of Freedom in Christ Ministries, tells us that when he conducted a "For Women Only" seminar in the early 1990s, "to my surprise most of the written questions dealt with sex in marriage. If I could synthesize their questions into one, it would be 'Do I have to do whatever my husband wants me to in bed?'" Tim LaHaye is even more blunt: "The sex drive in a man is almost volcanic in its latent ability to erupt at the slightest provocation." James Dobson, president of Focus on the Family, has said: "Many women stand in amazement at how regularly their husbands desire sexual intercourse." More recently, Paul Coughlin, in *No More Christian Nice Guy,* finds it rather irritating that evangelical wives were found—statistically—to be the most sexually satisfied wives in the nation. (He's invoking those early 1990s National Health and Social Life Survey research findings conducted by the University of Chicago team. Never mind that it was only 32 percent of conservative evangelical wives who always had orgasms during sex with their husbands versus a mere 27 percent among mainline Protestant and Catholic American women; no matter which number is considered, the findings were not exactly a ringing endorsement of the state of American heterosexuality. Yet the difference is still cause for right-wing pride.) But Coughlin is focused on something else. He thinks the untold story is that it's evangelical husbands who are not so satisfied. Coughlin complains vociferously about wives who give their husbands—who struggled so hard to preserve their own sexual purity in the midst of a sex-obsessed culture—nothing but the sexual equivalent of "frozen dinners" rather than the "fabulous banquets" they need and deserve. Coughlin says that "sex isn't the only reason some guys get married (at least it shouldn't be), but it's a biggie." And he regales readers with sad laments of husbands who suffer from being with wives who offer up "I'm-tired-so-hurry-up sex" or "did-I-detect-life? sex"—or even "new-car sex" or "bigger home sex"—when "what we really want and need is There's-No-One-Like-You sex." Coughlin may sound whiny, but he has an audience.

Again emphasizing the idea that women don't want sex as much as men, after reviewing the results of their survey of 1,300 individuals about the "top five love needs," evangelical syndicated radio talk-show hosts Dr. Gary and Barbara Rosberg—authors, individually and together, of at least a dozen books, including *Healing the Hurt in Your Marriage* and *Forty Unforgettable Dates with Your Mate*—make related observations. In their advice book on how best to *Divorce-Proof Your Marriage,* the Rosbergs relate that while for both spouses "unconditional love and acceptance" rank as number one, among husbands "sexual intimacy" is number two but does not even make it onto the wives' top-five list. The Rosbergs elaborate: "Much of a man's masculinity is rooted in his sexuality, a part of his maleness he cannot erase. As most couples discover, men spell intimacy S-E-X." The same cannot be said for his wife: "Wives spell intimacy T-A-L-K. For many women, conversation is the primary way they process thoughts, feelings, ideas, and problems."

The books in the "Every Man" series argue repeatedly that guys use emotions to get sex, while women use sex to get emotions. But the series takes this generic sentiment—so frequently asserted in mainstream culture as well—and amplifies it in wholly new ways. Arterburn's contention is that, put in the most rudimentary terms, if a husband can't do it to his wife every couple of days at least, he will stray—at least in his mind, if not with his body.

So what is the self-respecting evangelical wife supposed to do? This is where the quickie comes into play. It is also where some of the more disturbing aspects of evangelical advice come into the picture. For a woman has to be taught to cooperate. She must never ever compare her husband unfavorably to another man. The sin of comparison is as bad as the sin of sexual impurity. She should wear sexy lingerie, if he wants her to do so. But she must also give her husband sex whenever and however he wants it. For only in this way will her man be reassured. And a reassured husband is a satisfied husband and a satisfied husband is the key to marital bliss.

A central premise of *Every Man's Battle* is that men must learn to "bounce" their eyes. That is, they should practice and learn to look away immediately when confronted with a sexy image in the same way one would immediately yank a hand back from a hot stove. In this way, a guy can learn to "starve" his brain of all improper fantasies, memories, and images—anything and everything that is sexually stimulating that does not involve his wife. Stoeker and Arterburn recognize that Satan tempts men who will try this—and that the closer a man is to victory, the more Satan will develop ruses and rationalizations. But they express confidence that their step-by-step plan will work. They recommend going "cold turkey." Targeting masturbation alone won't work. The key is to target the eyes and mind. And then, in fact, there will be a huge—as they unabashedly say—"sexual payoff": "With your whole sexual being now focused upon your wife, sex with her will be so transformed that your satisfaction will explode off any known scale."

With reference to the husband who decides finally to give up the visual stimulations that fuel his sexual fantasies, Arterburn and Stoeker directly advise wives: "Once he tells you he's going cold turkey, be like a merciful vial of methadone for him. Increase your availability to him sexually, though this may be difficult for you since your husband might have told you some things that repulse you."

Wives are directly told to have sex with their husbands more often, no matter what it feels like for them. (All in the name of his sexual purity.) Having introduced their scientific conclusion that all men need to have their sperm released at least once in any seventy-two-hour cycle, Arterburn and Stoeker approvingly quote the testimony of "Ellen":

> In relation to your own husband, understanding the seventy-two-hour cycle can help you keep him satisfied. Ellen said: "his purity is extremely important to me, so I try to meet his needs so that he goes out each day with his cup full. During the earlier years, with much energy going into childcare and with my monthly cycle, it was a lot more difficult for me to do that. There weren't too many 'ideal times' when everything was just right. But that's life, and I did it anyway."

Voice-over interviews:

> So there's a place for the quickie. While a long-term diet of drive-by sex is unhealthy, it certainly has a place in defusing the power of the seventy-two-hour temptation cycle. Sometimes you just don't have the time or energy for the full package, but if you care about his purity, you can find just enough energy to get him by.

Evangelical women might be unhappy with their men—or with having sex with their men—but Arterburn and Stoeker argue that it is all for a good and godly cause. Take the case of "Andrea," again quoted by Arterburn and Stoeker: "Even if I'm tired or don't feel good, I can appreciate his sexual needs, so I do my part to satisfy him. I have to admit, though, I've had times that I felt resentful." Nonetheless, trooper that she is, Andrea soldiers on.

Sexual Problems:
A Common Side Effect of Combat-Related PTSD
Don Vaughan

The Warrior did his time in Iraq without complaint. For nine gru-
eling months, he accompanied his buddies on dangerous nighttime
raids, dodged IEDs hidden along war-ravaged roads, and engaged in
deadly firefights with frightening regularity. He killed enemy fight-
ers and watched, helpless and angry, as the enemy, in turn, killed or
maimed many of the men he had come to regard as brothers. At
night, in the dark, he prayed that he wouldn't be next.

When his commanding officer told him that he was finally going home, the Warrior was ecstatic. The reunion with his family
was so joyous that for two full weeks he barely thought about the
horrible things he had seen and done during his tour of duty as a
United State Marine.

Then the bright days started to turn gray. About a month after his return, the Warrior developed insomnia and other problems. His mind raced and his thoughts were plagued with the hor-

rible images of combat. Afraid and angry, he started drinking to dull the pain.

On the increasingly rare occasions when he felt like making love, the Warrior's body refused to cooperate. After a while, he stopped initiating intimacy with his wife because sex no longer brought him pleasure. The war in Iraq hadn't just taken the Warrior's peace of mind, it had robbed him of his sexuality as well.

Such stories are more common than you might assume among soldiers and Marines returning from Afghanistan and Iraq. In fact, according to Michael Russell, PhD, a noted clinical psychologist in San Antonio, Texas, who has more than twenty years of experience working with veterans and their families, within a year of returning from combat, one-third of all servicemembers will seek mental health assistance around a cluster of problems that include substance abuse, marital problems, depression, and full-blown posttraumatic stress disorder (PTSD).

"Every single one of these is associated with sexual dysfunction," Dr. Russell notes. "The best study to date, published in the *New England Journal of Medicine*, found PTSD rates of almost 20 percent in Marines and 18 percent in Army soldiers returning from combat deployments. That is a lot of people. And the literature suggests that one-third to one-half of those affected with an anxiety disorder like PTSD are going to have a concomitant sexual problem."

PTSD-related sexual dysfunction among veterans is nothing new. In fact, the Department of Defense and the Department of Veterans Affairs have been aware of the issue since the Vietnam era.

"I have been with the VA for about twenty years and I've been doing this kind of work the whole time," says William Finger, PhD, a clinical psychologist at the Mountain Home VA Medical Center in Mountain Home, Tennessee. "We have been well aware that there are sexual problems [within the veteran population]. We recognize this as a problem, we prioritize it as a treatment issue, and we have treatment programs available."

Unfortunately, says Dr. Russell, the sexual problems of many veterans often go unaddressed because both the patient and his or her health-care provider are uncomfortable bringing up the issue.

"I have noticed that sex problems sometimes suffer from 'don't ask, don't tell,' " Dr. Russell explains. "Doctors are embarrassed enough that they don't inquire about it and patients are embarrassed enough that they don't volunteer the fact that they are having a problem."

In addition, the military tends to foster a culture of machismo and a "tough it out" attitude that encourages servicemembers to hide their problems. "Admission of a sexual problem goes to the core of our perception as virile human beings," Dr. Russell notes. "Not surprisingly, too many veterans suffer in silence."

They're not the only ones, adds Eric Garrison, MAEd, MSc, a Manhattan-based sex counselor who has treated veterans with stress disorders. The issues of PTSD and sexuality also affect Army husbands, long-term partners, and gay, lesbian, and bisexual soldiers and their loved ones as well.

Indeed, it's important to note that war-related PTSD does not affect only men. Women have played a larger role in the wars in Iraq and Afghanistan than in any other conflict, and a good percentage of them are coming home with deep emotional wounds. Much of this psychological turmoil is the result of what they witnessed in theater, but some of it is also caused by conflicts with their fellow servicemembers.

"An important issue to keep in mind is military-related sexual trauma," observes Linda R. Mona, PhD, a licensed clinical psychologist in Los Angeles who has had experience with the veteran population. "Current research suggests that military sexual trauma is prevalent in both men and women who have served in Operation Iraqi Freedom (OIF) and Operation Enduring Freedom (OEF). Women face unique issues including the need to prove themselves to the men, having conflicts with other women, and experiencing a high rate of harassment, unwanted physical advances, and sexual assault. Not all women experiencing military sexual trauma will have PTSD, but some will."

In addition to PTSD, a variety of other issues can contribute to sexual problems among returning soldiers and Marines. One of the most common is the separation that comes with a lengthy deployment, notes Dr. Finger. These extended periods away from family, friends, and career can be especially difficult for National Guard and Reserve soldiers.

"Quite often, in their absence, their partners have had to step up to fill some of the roles the soldiers were filling before they left," Dr. Finger explains. "On the veteran's return, a lot of times those roles have to be renegotiated, which can create stress and result in disagreements and arguments, which in turn can have some impact on emotional intimacy, closeness, and the sexual relationship as well. That may be especially difficult for new relationships because some of those responsibilities haven't been clarified very well before deployment."

Another potential factor is a lack of communication while a soldier or Marine is in theater. Email and social networking sites such as MySpace have made staying in touch with family and friends easier than ever before, but service personnel often still find themselves out of communication for extended periods of time. This can wreak havoc with the emotions of service personnel and their loved ones back home, and affect sexual relationships upon a servicemember's return.

"Stress, anxiety, and other mood disorders can affect communication among couples as well as their ability to connect with each other sexually," notes Dr. Mona. "Being separated from one's partner and wondering whether or not you will ever see them again can place a great strain on a relationship. After being exposed to life-threatening trauma, some people may feel withdrawn, depressed, or anxious. These symptoms may prevent someone from engaging in social activities that were once pleasurable, interacting with family and friends, or feeling comfortable being sexual with their spouse or partner."

The meaning of sex may also change for individuals who have endured a life-altering experience, Dr. Mona adds. "Feeling guilty about surviving the war while others are still there is difficult," she explains. "Sexual relationships may become a lower priority."

Dr. Russell considers sexuality a barometer of the quality of a marriage. "When providing marital therapy, I always ask about frequency of sexual intercourse and satisfaction," he says. "The usual response, at best, is once or twice a week but many couples say it has been quite a while since their last encounter."

Veterans who have been traumatized during deployment may react to that stress in one of two ways: they either shut down their sexuality as a way of avoiding intimacy, or they develop a hyper-attachment to their partner. Both can have an adverse effect on a relationship, notes Patti Britton, PhD, a board-certified clinical sexologist, sexuality educator, and sex coach in Los Angeles.

"When someone sees friends blown up in front of them, as soldiers and Marines in Iraq and Afghanistan often do, it's natural to [pull back from relationships] in an attempt to avoid that kind of loss again," Dr. Britton explains. "This can occur even among those who are married and in a stable relationship because there's a perception of, 'Oh, I could lose him or her.' That's the shutdown.

"On the flip side, someone else may cope by really burrowing into an emotional relationship, an 'I never want to let her go' kind of thing, which can be strangulating in an emotional way. Both approaches can have a detrimental effect on relationships and on the formation of relationships."

Caregiving also carries certain concerns for both people with physical and psychological impairments and those family members who provide assistance. It is not uncommon for spouses and partners to develop a sense of frustration and helplessness as they try to assist their troubled significant other, who may have difficulty getting the care they now need.

"Even though an anxiety-based disorder is experienced by an individual, it can affect his or her entire family life," notes Dr. Mona. "Couples may have decreased communication patterns if the person experiencing PTSD shuts off verbally. However, some couples may actually strengthen their relationship out of this crisis. If the individual experiencing PTSD allows his/her partner in on this emotional experience, both emotional and physical intimacy can be sustained."

Another issue facing many returning veterans, and one that can have a formidable impact on sexuality, is that of body image, says Sandor Gardos, PhD, a licensed clinical psychologist and sex therapist in San Francisco. Body armor and improved field medicine save a far higher percentage of lives compared to past wars, but survivors often come home missing one or more limbs, or have extensive scarring, traumatic brain injury, and other aftereffects.

"These issues can result in dramatic changes in self-perception and self-identity," Dr. Gardos notes. "Coming home not looking and not feeling the same as you did when you left is going to have a tremendous impact on your sense of who you are sexually and how you interact with others."

"It's very difficult to be free sexually and experience sexual pleasure when you're hiding something about your body," agrees Dr. Britton. "Such issues pervade the culture at large but they become heightened and exaggerated when there is scarring, loss of a limb, or injury. More psychological and emotional healing may be required to accept the body as it is."

Physical injuries may also affect how an individual has sex, Dr. Britton adds. "For example, if a soldier comes home missing a leg and doggie-style is his and his wife's favorite position, it could be problematic because he can no longer easily assume that position," she explains.

"It becomes a matter of, 'Can I replicate this behavior and engage my partner in helping me do it, or has this been wiped out of our spectrum of how we can connect sexually?' " Dr. Britton notes. "Those are the kinds of important issues that must be faced."

The Department of Defense and the Veteran's Administration are stepping up to help. The wars in Afghanistan and Iraq have brought PTSD and the other debilitating effects of combat to the national forefront, and more is being done than ever before to prevent and treat them.

For example, servicemembers receive a mental health review prior to deployment, have access to mental health professionals in theater, and receive a mental health assessment within ninety days of their return home. In addition, the VA has greatly increased the number of mental health professionals on staff nationwide, and many VA centers have special OEF/OIF coordinators who look for and help servicemembers who may be struggling with their wartime experiences and/or the transition home.

"We have a whole team of people who go out and talk to soldiers, family members, and partners prior to deployment," confirms Dr. Finger. "They talk to them about the types of things they may experience when their family member is deployed and the types of available services that they can access while their family member is away.

"There is also a much greater emphasis on careful screening upon a soldier's return in regard to physical and mental health issues. There is much more effort to educate them about the types of services that are available. My understanding is that all returning OEF/OIF veterans have unrestricted access to health care for a minimum of two years to help them deal with anything related to their deployment. So there is a real effort to get them registered, identify their problems, and get them treated much more quickly."

Dr. Finger considers sexual issues the same as any other health or medical issue. "If a veteran brings up a sexual issue, it's going to be evaluated and addressed here," he notes. "And our providers are doing a much better job of actually making an effort to address those issues, to evaluate them and take care of them.

"That doesn't mean that every soldier who has a problem like this is going to report it. It's a sensitive, sometimes embarrassing topic and one that often is not brought up, even if a health-care provider asks. And if there is a problem, it may be denied. That's common."

When such barriers are broken down, say the experts, treatment for PTSD-related sexual dysfunction is usually quite successful. "If we can just cure the depression, rebuild the relationship a little bit, and keep the patient [from self-medicating with alcohol or drugs], he or she will usually be able to resume normal function," notes Dr. Russell. "Couples counseling with a good marital or sex therapist can also be very beneficial."

Nonetheless, if the Vietnam War is any indication, PTSD and its related side effects, including sexual dysfunction, are issues the Department of Defense and the VA will be struggling with long after the last soldiers return home from Afghanistan and Iraq.

"In many ways, the infrastructure is not in place right now to handle the sheer volume of disabled veterans coming back," observes Dr. Gardos. "Unless we make a concerted effort to expand available resources, we are going to have an entire generation of men and women who are scarred, both physically and psychologically, by their experiences. And this is going to have a devastating impact on their spouses and families. We cannot afford to ignore this problem and hope it will go away."

Dr. Britton agrees. "What we will discover is that [sexual dysfunction] will be a hidden epidemic that will be part of the fallout of these wars," she warns. "We will be dealing with this issue for many years to come."

Sources:

Michael Russell, PhD, a noted clinical psychologist in San Antonio, Texas, who has more than twenty years of experience working with veterans and their families. Tel: 210-221-7989. Email: michael. russell@amedd.army.mil.

William Finger, PhD, a clinical psychologist at the Mountain Home VA Medical Center in Mountain Home, Tennessee. Tel: 423-979-2934. Email: billfinger@yahoo.com; william.finger@med.va.gov.

Eric Garrison, MAEd, Msc, a Manhattan-based sex counselor who has treated veterans with stress disorders. Tel: 347-860-0809. Email: eric@ericgarrison.info.

Linda R. Mona, PhD, a licensed clinical psychologist in Los Angeles, who has had experience with the veteran population. Email: lrmona@aol.com.

Patti Britton, PhD, a board-certified clinical sexologist, sexuality educator, and sex coach in Los Angeles. Tel: 310-575-8889. Email: drpattixox@aol.com.

Sandor Gardos, PhD, a licensed clinical psychologist and sex therapist in San Francisco. Tel: 415-749-0942. Email: sgardos@ mypleasure.com.

Medpagetoday.com: "A Quarter of Iraq and Afghanistan Vets Show Mental Health Problems" by Neil Osterweil, March 12, 2007.

Penises I Have Known
Daphne Merkin

Sidling up to the Matter at Hand

There are penises so memorable that you never get over them: JC's for instance, a perfect edition worthy of my rapt contemplation, or so it seemed to me when I lay next to him on his seventies-style platform bed in his bachelor's pad on an unmemorable Manhattan side street years ago. Others, too, that you would like to recall—the one belonging to your first lover, for instance, the guy who "cracked your geode" (as the man in the red socks, another lover in your not inconsiderable lineup, once put it)—that seem to have eluded your visual grasp, through no fault of their own. Then again there are those that linger in you, like a ghost penis, although they are long gone, such as the impressive piece of equipment that came along with the deceptively slight fellow you met on a Jewish singles weekend at the now-defunct Grossinger's, a battering ram of a penis that left you raw, a penis so inflexible and obdurate that you could hang a towel on it—which, I might add, he did.

How to talk about your personal history with penises without sounding either all Mae West–bawdy (the old "Is that a gun in your pocket or are you just happy to see me?" routine) or all fluttery and awed, like a hitherto-untouched heroine in a bodice ripper (or, perhaps, like the touched-but-hitherto-unorgasmic heroine of D. H. Lawrence's *Lady Chatterley's Lover*), by the supernal otherness of the thing? "Now I know why men are so overbearing," Constance Chatterley says of her gamekeeper, Mellors, or more specifically of Mellors' penis, which he refers to as his "John Thomas," as though it were indeed an actual third person in the room, observing the action: "But he's lovely, *really*. Like another being! A bit terrifying! But lovely really!"

The problem, for starters, even before we get to the fact that it's difficult—impossible, even—for any single manifestation of this indubitably male organ to live up to its reputation, is how to deal with the word itself so that we're not all blushing or smirking. "Penis:" If you say it quickly, pass your eye over it glancingly as though it were not the quasi-scientific clunker of a word, you have accomplished nothing other than a grown-up game of peekaboo: I don't see you, big feller, bulging over there in the middle of the sentence. If, on the other hand, you give the thing its due and enunciate it fully, *pee-nus*, draw it out, acknowledge that it is an awkward coinage pretending to be at ease with itself under the enormous metaphoric burden it carries—bearing the weight of the phallocentric world between its legs—you are left having to deal with the (often incredulous) attention you have drawn by insisting that everything, but everything, is a stand-in for the phallic principle: cars, buildings, pencils, tails, fruit, revolvers, literary images. Take Dylan Thomas's "The force that through the green fuse drives the flower": it can be read as a poem about the life-giving power of a divine force, or,

BEST SEX WRITING 2009

in my view, it can be read as a poem about the life-giving force of penises, the surging motile energy of the male orgasm.

But here I am, getting stuck in an *apologia por vita erotica sua* before I have even begun. There are countless designations for "penis," of course, just as there are many terms for its equally klutzy-sounding female counterpart, the graceless "vagina." These designations include those one-syllable terms that sound like blunt, wham-bam-thank-you-ma'am heavy objects, such as "dick," "prick," and "cock," as well as the half-amused, half-abashed Yiddish approximations like "shmuck" and "putz." "Putz is worse than shmuck," Maggie Paley declares in her *The Book of the Penis*, which is a veritable font of information on points of lesser and greater interest, including the etymology of "penis," which is Latin for "tail" and a relatively late entry into the vernacular. She adds that the two terms "are now used almost entirely to mean 'jerk.'"

Then there are the many fancy descriptions of peckers that a certain kind of male writer delights in providing on behalf of his protagonist, such as Vladimir Nabokov's Humbert Humbert rendering his Lolita-avid penis in typically self-aggrandizing locution as the "scepter of my passion." James Joyce's Leopold Bloom, who hasn't had sex with his wife Molly in more than a decade, considers the generative potential lying dormant within his own relaxed endowment while lying in the bath ("limp father of thousands, a languid, floating flower") with a kind of endearing yet pathetic self-regard. And in Bellow's *Mr. Sammler's Planet*, Sammler comes face-to-face with a black pickpocket's "large tan-and-purple uncircumcised thing" only to find himself counterphobically fascinated with distinctions of color and creed: "Metallic hairs bristled at the thick base and the tip curled beyond the supporting, demonstrating hand, suggesting the fleshy mobility of an elephant's trunk, though the skin was somewhat iridescent rather than thick or rough." Not to overlook John Updike, who can always be counted on to sprinkle a few exactingly detailed, paint-by-number evocations of penises in each of his novels. In *Toward the End of Time*, there is a salute to the erect penis of the sex-preoccupied (but of course) narrator, who has masturbated himself to "full stretch" with the aid of his cache of pornography, the better to admire his own handwork: "the inverted lavender heart-shape of the glans, the majestic tensile column with its marblelike blue-green veins and triple-shafted underside. Stout and faithful fellow! My life's companion. I loved it, or him."

As for myself, I've always warmed to "Johnson," for some ineffable reason, just as I've always warmed to "cunt" over "pussy," for a similarly ineffable reason. And the ironic—or what I take to be ironic—majesty of "rod" speaks to the eighteenth-century serving girl in me. And yet, there is something about the word "penis" in all its obdurate two-syllabled out-thereness (I'll take one penis, if you please) that seems to rise above itself, if only because of the stiffly protruding quality of the first syllable (*pe*) followed by the curled-up flaccidity of the second (*nis*) seems to mimic the dynamic of charge and retreat that is embodied in the piece of male anatomy being alluded to.

Then again, what is this high-minded introductory musing on the strictures of a given lexicon—or, as is more likely, an extended patch of throat-clearing—but a symptom of the larger predicament of inarticulateness that I, an ordinarily voluble creature, find myself facing when in the presence of this subject? Despite their apparent demystification, penises themselves retain an odd aura of unspeakableness. For all the huge strides we appear to have taken in our discussion of *sex*—mainly by making it into a discussion about body and gender—the discourse doesn't seem to have advanced much since Lytton Strachey first dropped the word "semen" in one of those Bloomsbury discussions he and his friends, including Virginia Woolf (then Stephen) and her sister, Vanessa, used to have in one another's houses on London evenings in the early twentieth century. Which is why trying to talk about penises still feels, even after Erica Jong's zipless fuck, Monica Lewinsky, and "Sex in the City," like smashing through glass: as though one were daring to touch a precious and lovingly curated object behind its protective pane with the audacity of mere language. To talk about penises as a woman is to turn yourself into an outlaw and the conversation into smut even before we've gotten to the age-old question of whether size matters. Once and for all: it does, although in less significant and subtle ways than men think. Ernest Hemingway's infamously strutting account in *A Moveable Feast*, for instance, of being called upon to reassure F. Scott Fitzgerald that his equipment was adequate despite Zelda's ball-busting insinuations (the anecdote comes from a chapter with the insufferably coy title of "A Matter of Measurements") seems bogus on many accounts, not least of which is the suggestion that anxieties about the male-signifier-to-end-all-signifiers can be put to rest in quite so concrete a fashion. But the topic makes for easy send-up, as in the brand of condoms that offers a variety of prophylactics (the Nightcap, the Weekender, and the Extended Stay) all in boxes with the word *HUGE* printed on them.

Penises, it appears, deserve to be worshipped or envied (or, if need be, encouraged) but they don't deserve to be nattered on about. This is still sacred male territory and women trespass at their own literary peril. The potholes are everywhere you look, waiting to trip you up into porn or parody, or perhaps the high gutter baby talk of D. H. Lawrence. Which is not to suggest that Lawrence didn't, despite what is clearly a complicatedly ambivalent attitude toward women, manage to move the conversation more radically forward than most. There may be something laughable about the rhapsodic way Mellors and Lady Constance talk about his "John Thomas" in

Lady Chatterley's Lover, but there is also something both daring and poignant about Lawrence's attempt to win over his straitlaced and corseted readers to the liberating effect of erotic nakedness. His late phase especially, which includes *Lady Chatterley's Lover* and the short novel *The Man Who Died* (first published, by the bye, as *The Escaped Cock*), shows him pushing beyond what speculum-gazing Kate Millett and others have decried as his worship of the phallus into a more psychologically expansive view of carnal matters.

Lawrence was singular among his contemporaries for naming women's body parts and for attempting to depict female orgasm decades before Norman Mailer and Harold Brodkey got around to trying their hands at it. It seems all the more curious therefore that Virginia Woolf, in a speech she gave to an audience of two hundred women in January 1931 (almost a year after Lawrence's death), noted that it would take another fifty years before "men have become so civilized that they are not shocked when a woman speaks the truth about her body." Whether or not we have arrived at this juncture depends, I suppose, on your sense of how shockable we remain under our contemporary posture of jadedness, but please do note that Woolf's speculation does not make mention of a woman speaking the truth about *his* body. It is as though this were a possibility not even to be hinted at except on a different planet than ours. Which brings me back to where I began, unwilling to consign myself to the outpost of raunch yet unsure whether a seat will be found for me inside the clean, well-lit rooms of polite company.

The Matter at Hand

It is to be asserted, then, that very few women talk about the specifics of penises: the too-shortness, longness, thinness, fatness, curviness, redness, veininess, *whateverness* of them. Nice girls aren't supposed to take note of the individual penis in all its clinical details (its potential for beauty or hideousness as well as defining characteristics like length, girth, and color)—for fear, I suppose, that the whole delicate scaffolding, the prerequisite of a cock-of-the-walk confidence if a man is to be able to perform in the bedroom, would come crashing down around us.

Or perhaps it's simply that no one wants to know what her husband's or lover's penis really looks like when seen through the keyhole because it's too heavy a responsibility—like carrying around a state secret with you all the time, burning a hole in your pocket, imperiling future lives. An article I read in a woman's magazine about how to maintain strong friendships advised readers not to step over the other person's "comfort zone" and went on to cite a conversation about penis size—in which a friend of the writer's revealed in a whisper over lunch that the man she was dating and whom she would later marry had a very small penis ("It's, like, miniature")—as its first and most glaring example of an inappropriate revelation. The writer felt burdened with this indiscretion forever after and can't, apparently, see this friend alone or together with her minusculely endowed husband without feeling overcome with mortification.

Indeed, I have sophisticated female friends who to this very day continue to insist that there's no difference between one penis and the next. This claim always make me feel morally suspect, as though I were a foot fetishist or a frequenter of bondage chatrooms—someone mired in trivial and immature considerations, measuring the circumference of a banana while everyone else has moved on to worry about global warming. And, yes, I know that on the grander existential scale, or even on the less grand functional scale, it doesn't matter all that much, but then again neither does breast size or the shape of your ass—and men never tire of discussing these. One might conjecture that while the male gaze makes us feminine, confirms heterosexual women in their sense of their own desirability by the very act of assessing it (weighing breasts like so many sacks of potatoes and coming up with ideal ratios of waist-to-hip size as if women were Barbie dolls made real), the assessing female gaze *un*makes the masculine principle (the breast standing in for the woman, the penis for the man, rather than whole glorious beings)—He who does the Desiring. We in turn collude with men in treating the detached appraisal of sexual parts as an exclusively male prerogative by looking away and talking of the ardor or duration of men's sexual performance rather the prescribed nature of their equipment, whether crooked or straight, daunting or drooping.

Then again, there is no way not to take notice of what *is* more often than not first perceived to be an absurd and even ungainly appendage—before, that is, its emblematic significance to the human race is factored in, like bonus points for giving added Erector Set value. Not even I, brought up in an Orthodox German-Jewish household where my mother went wild if we failed to put on robes ("dressing gowns," as we called them) could successfully overlook the penises surrounding me. It's one thing to deliberately blind yourself to the reality of your father's penis—which, with the exception of girls who happen to be brought up around nudists, is what I think most of us do. To the extent that I wondered about my father's penis, I ascribed to it my feelings about him, which would have made his penis unlikable and scary at once (albeit not scary in a curiosity-inspiring way). But it's another thing altogether to overlook the penises of three brothers, especially if you happen to have slept in the same room with two of them until you are eight years old, at which point a psychiatrist suggests to your mother that it would be better for your already faltering mental health if you slept either by yourself or in a room with your two sisters.

I don't know whether I suffered from any adverse comparisons

I made between my own body and my brothers' bodies—whether, that is, I was affected by what used to go by the formal appellation "penis envy"—but I do know I felt outmuscled by them. And that I studied the crotches of their pajama pants when I thought no one was looking, intrigued by the odd way the cotton bunched up in this area—as though it contained a small cluster of grapes—while my own pajamas had to make no such accommodations. Years later I would be reminded of this disparity (and the fact that it had probably made more of an impression on me than I consciously realized) when I read one of Flaubert's tirades against the treacherous nature of women: "Women have no notion of rectitude. The best among them have no compunctions about listening at doors, unsealing letters, counseling and practicing a thousand little deceits, etc. It all goes back to their origin. Where man has an Eminence, they have a Hole! That eminence is Reason, Order, Science, the Phallus-Sun, and the hole is night, humidity, confusion." No wonder Madame Bovary gave up and swallowed arsenic.

And sometimes, it must be admitted, even *after* such calculations are made, after one has an idea of what penises can get up to, they still pose themselves as less than sublime. I think of a conversation I had not long ago, sitting around the kitchen table with my adolescent daughter and my forty-year-old Filipina housekeeper, concerning the physical noncharms of the penis. Of the three of us, I'm quite sure I was the only one who had seen an adult penis up close, and thus could draw on the vehicle of my senses rather than the evidence of visual images. But no matter: my daughter and my housekeeper were in cheerful agreement as to the unregenerate ugliness of penises—the sheer aesthetic silliness of the design, as they saw it, especially when you took into account the whole picture, including the surrounding hairiness and the existence of those two undignified balls.

I listened with some amusement to their remarks, envisioning us in a bawdy scene out of Chaucer, set in a dim low-ceilinged room lit by sputtering candles rather than in my linoleum-floored kitchen awash in recessed lighting, three girls sitting around the hearth speaking the unvarnished truth about men. (I should include my friend Elizabeth—who has been conversant in her time with a shuddersome number of penises and stoutly believes they're an acquired taste—in this warm and candid circle. "If you're a visual person," Elizabeth once explained to me, "the penis is a hideous organ, which isn't to say I don't like them.") But I also felt a slight sense of unease, even foreboding, at the dismissive tone that was being taken. What, I wondered, if men (any man, the father of three across the hall, say, or the doorman who guarded us from potential marauders and always greeted us as though he was genuinely happy to see us again) knew that they were being viewed in this way— that it was even possible to size up their most prized credential with so much irreverence? I understood that my unmarried and possibly virginal housekeeper had little use for men, but how had I failed in transmitting to my daughter the necessary sense of gravitas about the subject, without which she would clearly be doomed, giving off the wrong signal, a slew of insufficiently dazzled pheromones?

It wasn't, after all, as though I were consciously trying to raise a rampaging shrew, a Lorena Bobbitt, say, or, going back several decades, a maddened man hater like Valerie Solanas, who first penned the *SCUM Manifesto* and then shot Andy Warhol. Heaven forfend. I had loved men in my time, including my daughter's father; I had loved penises, sometimes more than the men they were attached to. Presumably I would do so again, but meanwhile I saw the line I had to adopt. It was up to me to put matters right, to defend the maligned organ. "It's actually quite nice," I heard myself say, as we all scraped the last of the mint-chocolate-chip ice cream from our bowls. I moved gingerly from the particular to the general, trying to walk a line between a discriminating embrace and wholehearted sluttishness: "They sort of grow on you." And then, as the coup de grace, I, who had gone through life half resistant and half in thrall to men and their effect on me, especially in bed, who had resisted the "privileging" of the male sexual organ even as I marveled at its ability to transform itself from something soft and passive into something hard and driven and capable of filling you up like a stopper in a bottle, came out openly as an advocate. As my daughter and my housekeeper first stared at me and then at each other, I added: "I like them." Just in the nick of time, I retracted a bit, lest I sound like I was a come-one-come-all appreciator of penises, the sort of woman who liked all flavors of ice cream as long as they were cold. "I mean, some of them."

The Matter in Hand

Sooner or later it happens. They exert their charms; persuade you that your Hole needs their Eminence. Or if not quite that, they prove indispensable to your feeling more vivid and less alone, no longer adrift in the vastness of the world but grounded in the snug fit of the erotic moment. In my case, the pivotal "Aha!" arrived, in the manner of many belated recognitions, with a compensatory force, so that for a while in the latter half of my twenties I found myself walking around in a haze of penis longing. After holding on to my virginity until the age of twenty-five with a slightly deranged fervor indicative of equal parts fear and desire, I acted as though I had awakened to a new morning. The world seemed charged not with the grandeur of God, as the poet Gerard Manley Hopkins had it, but with the grandeur of erections. I liked the feel of a penis growing firm in my hand (it would take years before I felt truly comfortable with a penis in my mouth), and I loved the feel of an urgent penis inside me, pushing through beyond my usual barriers to the hopelessly receptive Lady Chatterley core of me. I thought they—the confederacy of penises—were close to amazing in their ability to change shape in so dramatic a way. I imagined it to be a special effect that kept happening just for me, over and over again. It was hard for me to believe that other women—scads of other women—could produce this same result.

The penises I became acquainted with were uniformly circumcised—I had wandered away from my religiously observant upbringing, but not that far—and early on I noticed small differences between one circumcised penis and another that turned out not to be so small. There were a few times I got out of bed midway because the penis in question was too big or too stocky or hazardously curved, like a scimitar. Once I fled the Plaza Hotel because a minor movie producer with a legendary reputation as a cocksman appeared not only to be hung like the proverbial horse but had a slightly glazed look in his eye, which, together with his musings on the wonders of anal sex, scared me back into my clothes. Several years later, when this same man and I went to bed in a hotel in Beverly Hills, I felt appreciative of the vigor with which he made love, his penis no longer striking me as gargantuan but rather as generous.

I remember watching afterward as he sat naked on the edge of the capacious hotel bed, singing some ditty he had learned in military school decades earlier. He began to get dressed by pulling on a pair of red socks and for a moment, before he put on the rest of his clothes, I felt a great sense of loss. He was leaving me in my expensive room—taking his penis, which I had become fond of, with him. For a moment, I thought of asking him to stay, or of asking him to leave me his penis as a memento. We women become quite attached, you know, which is both our triumph and our defeat. If I had to make a guess as to what it is that we become attached to I would end up fumbling for the right words, talking in slightly abject terms about the feeling of being filled, which sounds suspiciously as though I believed in Flaubert's antiphonal Holes and Eminences, when what I really believe in is something vaguer, something along the lines of a certain kind of need being met by a certain kind of virile understanding. Not to get too Lawrentian about it, I suppose I might say that we are all composed of psychological Holes and Eminences and that sometimes a man comes along wearing the red socks—or maybe it's really the penis by way of the red socks—you've been looking for all these years. At which point you're a goner and his penis, whatever its reality, looks like the very model you've been lusting after without even knowing it.

Sex Is the Most Stressful Thing in the Universe
Dan Vebber

When I was a child, sex was awesome. Of course, when I was a child, I didn't have to deal with it. Sex was what Dan of the Future would one day enjoy, and I saw no reason to obsess about it any more than Present-Day Dan obsesses with...what's something old people enjoy? Nice breezes. Let's say nice breezes.

In fact, I never beat off as a kid. I didn't beat off thinking about girls, I didn't beat off thinking about boys, I didn't even beat off thinking about spaceships. (This is the point at which people quote me HILARIOUS statistics along the lines of "99 percent of teenage boys masturbate, and 1 percent are liars!" HA! Thank you for your opinion, please return to hosting your Morning Zoo program.) The fact is, not once during my outwardly normal adolescence could I dupe my machinery into getting physically aroused by the mere thought of sex, the touch of my own hand, or porn. (Not every guy has a longstanding and storied relationship with porn. Some of us honestly don't find it interesting enough to warrant looking past the girls' bad teeth.)

When I was seventeen, I started dating Molly Malone. I've changed her name here, but not her full-blooded Irish ethnicity or any of the attendant baggage that implies. Catholic? Check. Shocking red hair and freckles? Check. Overbearing, shillelagh-waving father? Double check. Our senior year of high school, Molly and I were inseparable, and at least as far as the sex thing went, we were perfect for each other: She didn't want to lose her virginity because of her Catholic guilt, and my retarded libido wasn't compelling me to pressure her into it. She was my first real love, breaking through my veneer of irony and cynicism to the point where I actually enjoyed squiring her to a prom with the odious theme "Knights in White Satin."

Molly was a brilliant girl, and translated that brilliance into acceptance to no less of a prominent Ivy League institution than Havrard University. (I have flipped the third and fourth letters of the school's name to further protect identity.) This is where things started to fall apart, as Molly became increasingly obsessed with the notion that she, with her love of deconstructing wordplay in French poetry, was much smarter than me, with my love of deconstructing the comedic premise behind David Letterman wearing a suit made of Alka-Seltzer. One night we were making out and listening to XTC's "The Mayor of Simpleton," the lyrics of which are a plea from an idiot to a brainy girl along the lines of "I may not be well versed in any topics that would gain me admiration among the intelligentsia, but the one thing I DO know is that I love you." Delighted, Molly pointed out to me, "Aww, it's a song about us!" At the time I took the comment in the spirit of playfulness that was likely intended. But years later, looking back...Jesus! What the fuck was that? More importantly, what the fuck was wrong with

ME that I was so wiling to put up with a girlfriend who repeatedly hammered into my head that I was a dumbass?

Being a brainless troglodyte, I ended up in Madison at the University of Wisconsin. My existence became an endless blur of dorm-room keggers, advocacy journalism, and focusing my abnormally large reserves of vitriol on fellow students dumb enough to be vexed by the question, "But is it art?" Clarity only seemed possible during the times when Molly and I would visit each other. As these dorm-room visits were the first time we had access to unsupervised beds, we'd spend a lot of time sleeping together. Though for us "sleeping together" was merely the next logical step on our path toward sexual intercourse, as opposed to a euphemism for it. The mere insertion of parts into other parts would have seemed anticlimactic after an evening spent solving the Gordian knot of balancing two sleeping bodies on a single mattress, waking up with severely restricted blood flow in at least one limb, and overlooking each other's post-Chinese-food morning breath.

As magical as those visits with Molly were, the time spent apart from her became that much more unbearable. This wasn't helped by the fact that Molly was acting totally unreasonably at her new school, engaging in conversations with guys who weren't me and attempting to join social groups that weren't made up of me, me, and me. On some Friday nights she would even choose to attend a book club or act in a play rather than sit alone by her phone waiting for my sobbing call. How could one girl be so heartless?

Our dance of dysfunction and lack of sex continued throughout our freshman and sophomore years. We called the whole thing off more times than I can remember, and usually for reasons that were entirely my fault. The ratio of time spent long-distance dating to time spent long-distance broken up gradually decreased, until we agreed to acknowledge what geography had been screaming at us for months: we were no longer together.

The spring of 1991, my junior year, was an exciting time. I had a dorm room to myself, I was drawing a well-regarded daily comic strip for my school paper, and Our Troops had just finished kicking Saddam's ass in the first Gulf War, setting the stage for the peace in the Middle East we enjoy to this day. I had moved on from Molly and was a better man for it, though my inexperience with sex was starting to be a problem. The girls I dated wanted more than a smooch and a boob kneading to top off their night. "We should wait until we're ready," I'd declare, usually succeeding in convincing potential partners that I was a sensitive and decent man as opposed to a tragically repressed and inexperienced boy. The problem with this tactic was that a girl, once flattened by my tsunami of sensitive decency, would fall for me even harder, making it that much more difficult to dump her when my well of excuses for putting off sex finally ran dry. Their faces haunt me to this day: the suburban punker who worked the counter at the record store, the doe-eyed lifeguard certified in massage, the perky art chick who scraped up roadkill and used it in an installation piece... They were nerdy goddesses all, but I could never make a relationship with them last more than a couple weeks, and I was starting to hate myself for it. Such was my state of mind when Molly called me out of nowhere and requested I fly to Boston for the express purpose of having sex.

The specific circumstances surrounding Molly's offer of virginity loss are admittedly fuzzy, and largely rooted in emotion. But what I do remember with the clarity of tropical fish footage on a Best Buy showroom HDTV is that we were definitely, definitely not in love anymore. Knowing this, I was overcome with the absolute certainty that this "orgasm-or-bust" odyssey could not possibly end in anything but disaster and embarrassment for both of us. I bought the first plane ticket I could find.

Once I arrived at Havrard, Molly and I went straight to work constructing the infrastructure she deemed necessary for "safe sex." This consisted of four forms of birth control, which, per Molly's instructions, would need to be utilized simultaneously.

One: The Rhythm Method

There was a window of three or four days in Molly's cycle that she had calculated to be "safe." That window didn't open until a couple days into my visit, so we killed time, probably walking the Freedom Trail or some shit.

Two: Condoms

We went to purchase these together, studying the boxes until we were confident we'd found the thickest, least comfortable, most spermicide-drenched contraceptives science could produce.

Three: The Sponge

I'm thirty-seven and I still don't know quite how these are supposed to work. More on this later.

Four: The Number-One Rule

"DO NOT ejaculate while inside me! Pull out the second you think it's getting dangerous."

In retrospect, she may not have wanted to get pregnant.

Beginning with her phone call, and throughout our quest to purchase birth control, Molly's constant mantra was, "We've got to get this over with." Is there any sentence in the English language that conveys less passion or romance? Thanks to the last moments leading up to our attempt at sex, Molly provided me with at least one: "Just so you know, this is going to be really painful for me, and I'm probably going to be bleeding all over the place." This final sweet nothing imparted, and the fortress of contraception having been built (including Molly's mood-killing last-minute dash behind a closed bathroom door so she could have privacy as she put the sponge in), it was finally time for me to get a boner and fuck my way into adulthood. Three, two, one…go! Go! The light is green! The ref fired his starter pistol! Cut the yellow wire RIGHT NOW or the bomb goes off!

It didn't take Molly long to notice something was up, or more accurately, wasn't. After all, whenever we had gone at it with the unstated understanding that no sex was forthcoming, I'd grow a cop's flashlight in my pants. (My point is not to imply that I have a particularly large penis, but simply to state via colorful metaphor that my boners came more easily when I wasn't picturing Molly bleeding to death.) Molly's reaction to my lack of stiffness was, at first, sympathetic, if confused ("It's okay. Take your time…"), but quickly snowballed into impatient, nastier territory ("I'M doing everything right. What's wrong with YOU?"). After a couple of futile hours of frustration, hair pulling, and being flat-out belittled by My Wild Irish Rose, I put on my clothes and exited Molly's dorm room into the drizzly Havrard night, alone.

On that walk, I ate half a bag of white-cheddar popcorn and came to the conclusion that would screw me up forever: I was incapable of having sex. Never mind that no one but the randiest of porn stars would have been able to get it up amidst the shitstorm of stress, fear, and inexperience I was dealing with. Such logical explanations were obliterated by my feelings of failure and shame, compounded by Molly's anger that her virginity problem wouldn't be solved anytime soon.

The next night we went to a party, where I embarrassed Molly by conversing with one of her more bearable friends about our shared obsession with the band Devo. "These people go to Havrard! They don't want to talk about stupid shit like Devo!" Molly screamed. I, in turn, exploded at her flat-out wrong assessment of her friend's degree of interest in Akron's proudest sons, and suddenly we were in the fight that ended our relationship once and for all. We agreed to avoid each other over the six remaining days of my trip. (Why I didn't just fly home on an earlier flight is lost to the mists of time, but knowing me, I probably didn't want to inconvenience the airline.) I spent my nights freezing on Molly's couch, and my days reading Vonnegut outside an Au Bon Pain. I think I may have had a nervous breakdown at some point, as I distinctly remember curling up next to Molly's dorm-room fireplace, sobbing uncontrollably about nothing and everything. (And what kind of bullshit dorm room has a fireplace in it, anyway? Fuck Havrard.)

In the end, after all we went through, the most enduring lesson I learned from Molly is that regardless of whether or not my parts work on a given try, sex is always the most stressful thing in the history of the universe. After (and because of) our failed attempt at Sin, it took me three more years to officially lose my virginity. And to this day, despite being blissfully married and having fathered a kick-ass son, I consider myself a victim of Post-Traumatic Sex Disorder. (If I've inadvertently stolen this from a struggling stand-up comedian, I humbly apologize.) Every single sexual encounter of my life has been preceded by feelings of overwhelming dread, because no matter how many hundreds of times I've hardened up and rocked it in there, part of me is still that confused twenty-year-old, staring at my flaccid shame, getting berated for being defective. Worse still, the mere whiff of white-cheddar popcorn still brings back all the hopeless feelings I went through in the rain that night almost twenty years ago. And I used to love that shit!

I did, however, learn to masturbate at age twenty-four, making me the only man on Earth to lose his virginity to a girl before losing it to himself. And if that fact doesn't bring a tear of hope to your eye, then I'm sorry, but you simply aren't human.

Silver-Balling
Stacey D'Erasmo

So Beth and I are lying around in bed one morning, next to the computer. We get an email from our friend Troy that reads, in part, *St. James will be at the party if he isn't too busy silver-balling his hot new boyfriend.*

Beth and I look at each other. "What's silver-balling?" I say.

She says, "I don't know. Something with Christmas ornaments?"

We go out to dinner with Paul and George. Before the appetizers arrive, I say, "Hey. What's silver-balling?"

Paul looks abashed. "Silver-balling? Silver-balling?"

"I've never heard of that," says George.

Paul says, "I think it's when you're old and you have sex. Like having sex with silver foxes."

"What are silver foxes?" Beth asks.

"You don't know what silver foxes are?" says George.

Beth shakes her head.

"Hmm," says George.

"It's being old," says Paul. "And having sex with men."

"You're lying," I say. "You don't know what silver-balling is."

"Do, too," says Paul.

I write our friends Katie and Liz and Jill with the subject heading "silver-balling." Katie writes back, *What the fuck is that? You dip them in silver? Who would do that?*

I ask my friend Adrian when she comes back from her date with the Frenchman. She says confidently, "Oh, it's ben wa balls. Definitely. You know, those balls you insert and then pull out slowly? They're silver. That's silver-balling."

"Does it matter where you insert them?" I ask.

"Nope," she says.

I ask my friend Linda if she knows what silver-balling is. *I'm trying to figure out if I've done it,* she writes back. *Have I? Have you?*

I'm not sure. I Google it. One definition appears to be "killing people"—i.e., shooting them. The term also turns up in a porn DVD description of something done in a "stall." A horse stall? A bathroom stall? The urban slang dictionary offers that it means: *when you skeet skeet skeet in your girlfriend's mouth and she spits it on your balls.* Okay, possible, though not, perhaps, the last word. All other uses of the word have to do with jewelry. Perhaps it means hanging jewelry all over someone in a horse stall and then shooting that person? Or "shooting" on that person? I know James only slightly, but I can't quite see him doing that. Also, he doesn't have a horse, or a horse stall, as far as I know.

Beth and I are perplexed, and embarrassed, and we still don't know if either of us has done it, or not, and do we want to do it? This silver-balling? Whatever it is, I notice that I like to say it, that there is some sort of erotic charge in the sound of those *s*'s and *l*'s, that hard little *b* rolling around on the tongue, the slippery and receptive gerund, the invocation of silver shockingly close to the tenderness of balls—ouch!—the proximity of metal to flesh, the glamour of the juxtaposition of silver and skin. I don't know if I've done silver-balling, but after a few days I know that I have, at least, said and written *silver-balling,* and the more I say it, the hotter it gets. Beth and I say it quite a bit, and we ask nearly everyone we know about it, with the exception of Troy. We don't ask Troy because we don't want the silver-balling game to end yet. No one, it turns out, knows what it is, and we discover that there is a pleasure in that, too: the erotic unknown. Surprising your friends, who like to think they are sexually sophisticated, with an act they've never heard of and that is possibly injurious. Like Catherine Deneuve opening the buzzing box in the Buñuel film *Belle du Jour,* that box of erotic mystery. What's in there? Why is it buzzing? Why does she look so happy when she opens it?

Silver-balling. Say it a few times. See what I mean? It's Seussian, also a bit Marie Antoinette. One can imagine they were silver-balling at Versailles. Lucky James, to be silver-balling said hot new boyfriend. It kind of turns me on that I can't quite see what they're doing in there, that the shadows don't make sense to me. In my mind, the silver is molten, but also cool, which isn't possible in reality. In my mind, silver-balling is special, dangerous, complex.

After a week or so, Beth and I finally give in and write Troy. *What is silver-balling? Oh,* he writes back, *I just made that up. I have no idea.*

Silver-balling. Silver-balling. Silver-balling. It rings in the mind, full of promise.

Sex Dolls for the Twenty-First Century
David Levy

By the early 1980s, blow-up sex dolls were becoming quite big business in some countries but were viewed as obscene in others. In 1982 David Sullivan, a British sex entrepreneur, attempted to import from West Germany a consignment of inflatable rubber dolls. When inflated, these became life-size replicas of a woman's body, complete with the usual three orifices to provide male customers with sexual gratification. The dolls were seized by the British Customs and Excise as "indecent or obscene articles" and their seizure was upheld in the condemnation proceedings before magistrates and on appeal to the Crown Court. But Sullivan's company, Conegate, then appealed to the High Court in Britain, and, having lost that appeal as well, Conegate appealed yet again, this time to the European Court of Justice, where finally the company won the case in 1987. It turned out that the English law prohibiting the importation of the dolls, which dated from 1876, had been superseded by articles 30 and 36 of the 1957 Treaty of Rome, the document signed when the European Economic Community was created. Under the terms of the treaty, restricting the importation of the dolls into the United Kingdom would have constituted an arbitrary barrier to free trade, and it was free trade that the treaty was specifically designed to promote. The major consequence for the British government of losing this case was that *all* import restrictions on "obscene or indecent" items had to be lifted!

The paucity of published information on the history of sex dolls makes it extremely difficult to date the launch of the first products that appeared on the market in commercially interesting quantities, though the Conegate case indicates that it must have been no later than 1982. Since the mid-1990s at least, various grades of sex doll have been manufactured, ranging from inexpensive inflatable welded-vinyl models, whose looks leave much to be desired but which incorporate an artificial vagina—the main purpose of their customers—through midpriced products made of heavy latex and with convincingly molded hands and feet, imitation eyes in glass or plastic, and styled wigs adorning their mannequin-like heads; up to the top-of-the-line products that in 2006 cost in the region of $7,000, such as the market leader in this price range—RealDoll.

It was in 1996 that Matt McMullen, a California sculptor, revolutionized the sex-toy industry when he launched Nina, the first of a line of products sold under the RealDoll brand name by his company, Abyss Creations. McMullen had previously worked in a Halloween-mask factory, making innocent sculpted female forms in his spare time as a sideline. These were mostly small figures, about twelve inches tall, made of resin and sold as models. With time he began to make larger dolls and to use materials that were softer to the touch. He also designed a skeleton in order to allow his dolls to have limbs that could move.

When McMullen started to advertise his dolls with photographs on his website, he received several inquiries from people who believed his products to be sex dolls. When he explained to them that they were wrong, the inquiries changed to ones asking him if he would manufacture sex dolls, a group of visitors to his site offering him three thousand dollars each for ten dolls. So he quit his job at the mask factory, developed a silicone material that could be employed to make the doll's genitalia durable and feel right, and by 1996 he was in business.

The RealDoll products are lifelike in appearance as well as being life size and close to life weight. The nine different body sizes advertised on the RealDoll site in early 2006 ranged from five feet one inch tall to five feet ten; they weighed in at between seventy and one hundred pounds; they offered busts from 34A to 44FF, waists from twenty-two to twenty-six inches, and hips from thirty-four to thirty-eight. Other available options included fourteen different female heads, each with its own name: Amanda, Angela, Anna Mae, Brittany, Celine, et al.; seven shades of hair coloring; six different colors for the eyes; fair, medium, tanned, Asian, or African skin tones; and red, blonde, or brunette pubic hair that can come shaved, trimmed, or "natural." The dolls are based around articulated skeletons made of steel, have artificial elastic flesh made of silicone, and they come with three functioning "pleasure portals"—vagina, oral, and anal. Each female doll is thus custom-made, with the buyer able to choose from more than 500 million permutations of these various options.

In addition to the fourteen female models for sale early in 2006, one model of a male doll was also available. It was named Charlie—five feet ten inches tall, with a forty-four-inch chest, a thirty-two-inch waist, and a stocky body. Charlie was priced at $7,000 plus shipping charges and could be provided with "anal entry if desired, plus one size of penis attachment," size not specified. The female RealDolls at that time were slightly less expensive, at $6,500 dollars, and the company was talking of sales in the region of 300 to 350 per year.

RealDoll is by no means the only American brand on the market. A rival California company, CyberOrgasMatrix, uses a different body material—an elastic gel that the manufacturers claim is stronger and more realistic than silicone, as well as being less expensive. Their principal product is the Pandora Peaks model, which, like RealDoll, comes with numerous options. Customers pay according to which options they choose, so that, for example, while vaginal and oral entries are standard, anal entry costs an extra $250. Yet another California manufacturer is SuperBabe, whose doll is modeled on the porn star Vanessa Lace.

The number of sex-doll manufacturers is increasing steadily, as are the websites that sell them.[1] And not to be outdone by the growing band of American producers, companies in China, Germany, and Japan have been getting in on the act. In Nuremberg, Germany, an aircraft mechanic named Michael Harriman claims to have created the world's most sophisticated sex doll, called Andy, with skin made from a silicone-based material employed in plastic surgery, an artificial heart that beats harder during sex, in time with the doll's harder breathing, which stays cold just as in real life. Andy can be made to move by remote control, wiggling her hips under the sheets and making other suggestive movements, all at the touch of a button. The price is similar to that of RealDolls, but there are additional charges for special modifications, such as extra-large breasts. Harriman claims that his dolls "are almost impossible to distinguish from the real thing, but I am still developing improvements and I will only be happy when what I have is better than the real thing."

A wide assortment of Chinese offerings is available online and in sex shops, at prices ranging from $50 to $250, as described by Meghan Laslocky:

> Sweet Spot: A Taste of Things to Come, a catalogue from Hong Kong, lists nearly 70 different models of blow-up doll, including saucy Sondrine, whose hair, nipples, and genitalia glow in the dark; Betty Fat Girl Bouncer, to satisfy the chubby chaser; Brandi Sommer, with "super vibrating LoveCline™ lips"; and the Perfect Date, which is just 36 inches tall and is equipped with a mouth and cup holder built into her head. There's even a dairy maid doll who lactates and has short blonde braids reminiscent of Swiss Miss. Some of the blow-ups vibrate and, oddly enough, scream.

Thus have the sexual lives of sailors, among others, been enriched with the advances in doll design and materials technology, advances that have created realistic skinlike substances such as "CyberSkin"[2] and have thereby made the current generation of sex dolls more comfortable to use than earlier models. That sailors are still avid patrons of such products is of little doubt, and an interesting example of their use was described by Ellen Kleist and Harald Moi in a learned journal in 1993. This report involved the skipper of a fishing trawler from Greenland. After some three months at sea, the skipper had occasion to rouse the ship's engineer in his cabin during the night because of engine trouble. After the engineer left his cabin to sort out the problem, the skipper observed a bump in the engineer's bed, whereupon he found an inflatable doll with an artificial vagina and was tempted into using it in order to assuage his sexual starvation. A few days after this episode, the captain experienced a discharge from his penis, and upon the trawler's return to port in Greenland he sought advice at a hospital in Nanortalik. There had been no women on board the trawler while it was at sea; the skipper denied having had any homosexual contacts, and there was no doubt in the minds of the doctors that the onset of the symptoms was more than two months after leaving port, which meant that the source had to have been on board the trawler. The engineer was then examined by the hospital doctors and found to have gonorrhea. He had observed a mild discharge from his own penis after the ship left port but had not been treated with antibiotics. He admitted having ejaculated into the vagina of the doll just before the skipper had called on him, without washing the doll afterward. He also admitted having sex with a girl some days before the trawler put to sea. Kleist and Moi's account in *Genitourinary Medicine*[3] suggests that this was the first reported case of the transmission of gonorrhea through an inflatable doll.

The marketing of RealDolls and their cousins from other manufacturers tends to be based on the idea that they are "the perfect woman," perfect because they're always ready and available, because they provide all the benefits of a human female partner without any of the complications involved with human relationships, and because they make no demands on their owners, with no conversation and no foreplay required. And it is precisely because of these attributes, the doll's lack of "complications" and demands, that they will likely appeal to many of the men who gave such explanations as to why they pay prostitutes for sex, and to others who have similar feelings about their sex lives at home. So, already, in this promotional slant, we can see the basis of the idea that men who use prostitutes should save up their dollars until they can afford a RealDoll. I believe that this will happen in a big way, and that the New York hooker who feared that robot technology would decimate her profession will be proved correct. The signs are already there, as you will soon see.

The most successful manufacturer of sex dolls in Japan is Orient Industries, whose president, Hideo Tsuchiya, started working in the adult sex-aid business in the early 1960s, opening his own store shortly afterward. His business boomed fairly quickly, due largely to two dolls, named Antarctica 1 and Antarctica 2, that achieved media fame of a sort when some of Japan's scientists took them as companions for the winter at Showa Base, Japan's headquarters in Antarctica. At that time Tsuchiya's dolls had permanently open mouths and were inflatable. Although sales were brisk, the blow-up dolls had a tendency to develop leaks and would often burst under the weight of their owners. So Tsuchiya decided that he needed a more durable product, which he achieved by using stronger materials and a design that did not need to be inflated. One of the company's early models, called "Omokage," was specially designed to be dismantled into lower and upper portions, for easy storage in the cramped space of Japan's traditionally small homes.

The growing success of the dolls manufactured by Orient Industries was reported in the *Mainichi Daily News* in late 2003.[4] "Early on, the showroom was more like a therapy area," recounted Tsuchiya. "We'd get old guys who had permission from their wives to buy dolls, or mothers of disabled sons searching for a partner. Nearly all of our customers had some problem related to their sex life."

As the popularity of sex dolls in Japan increased, the attitude of customers toward their dolls transformed, from their being "considered mere instruments in which men could ejaculate to objects of deep affection." By late 2003, Tsuchiya's dolls were selling so well that he was able to boast how it took only ten minutes for fifty new dolls to disappear from the shelves. Standing just under five feet tall and weighing around fifty-seven pounds, the sale of the

Orient Industries dolls was beginning to become a fairly big business, increasingly attracting attention from the media. In one report by *Dacapo*[5] journalist Mark Schreiber that appeared in a 2004 edition of *Asian Sex Gazette*,[6] Tsuchiya revealed how "Dutch wives,"[7] as they are called in Japan, have their own special place and treatment within the confines of Japanese culture, with discarded dolls having the opportunity of funeral rituals redolent of the virtual cemeteries devised for "dead" Tamagotchis.

"A Dutch wife is not merely a doll, or an object. She can be an irreplaceable lover, who provides a sense of emotional healing." Speaking at his showroom near JR Okachimachi Station, where some two dozen of Orient Industries' ersatz females are displayed, Tsuchiya tells *Dacapo*'s reporter that for years his clientele had typically been handicapped men, or single men over forty. But from around six years ago, when he commenced sales via the Internet (www.orient-doll.com), he was mildly surprised to receive a surge of orders from men in their twenties and thirties.

"When I ran my hand along the doll's thighs," confesses *Dacapo*'s reporter, "I felt a shiver of excitement." After observing the painstaking effort that goes into the making of each doll at Orient Industries' factory, the reporter came away enlightened. "Many people might be inclined to disparage sex toys," he writes, "but these dolls truly exemplify Japan's status as a high-tech country!"

Jewel and her sisters are shipped to purchasers in cardboard boxes stamped *kenko kigu* (health apparatus), and users are assured of lifelong after-service. As the vow "Until death do us part" may be stretching things a bit, the company anticipates a time when Jewel might outlive her usefulness or her owner. "If a *yome* [bride] is no longer needed, we'll disretely [*sic*] take her off a customer's hands at no charge," Tsuchiya adds. "Twice a year we also arrange for a *kuyo* [Buddhist memorial service] for discarded dolls at the special bodhisattva for dolls at the Shimizu Kannondeo in Ueno Park." Founded in 1631, it's where the "souls" of dolls are consecrated. (Kannon is the Goddess of Mercy.)

A few months after this *Asian Sex Gazette* article appeared, a small group of Japanese entrepreneurs, who had previously been thinking of starting up a regular escort service, decided instead to hire out sex dolls rather than young women. In August 2004 their company, *Doll no Mori* (Forest of Dolls), opened its first shop in Tokyo's Ota district, specializing in deliveries of dolls to hotels as well as to private homes. Initially *Doll no Mori* was renting out to around twenty customers per month, but by April 2005 their first shop had increased its customer base to one hundred and fifty per month, and the business had been franchised to forty other shops nationwide, with monthly turnovers averaging anywhere from $2,500 and $25,000 per shop. The company's manager, Hajime Kimura, explained to the newspaper *Nikkan Gendai* that although "we expected most of the clients to be *eotaku* (geeky) types, as it turned out, most of them are ordinary salarymen in their 30s and 40s." For customers who wish to dress up their dolls, there are optional extras at around $80 each, including wigs, negligees, bathing suits, and other costumes such as school uniforms and French maids' outfits. In a follow-up article in *Nikkan Gendai,* sex therapist Kim Myung Gun explained, "People have been saying for a long time that men have lost their desire for real women. Rather than have sex with a woman who doesn't fulfill their expectations, they would rather play with something that corresponds to their fantasy, even if she's not real."

It quickly became clear in Japan that the fembot's far less technologically sophisticated ancestor, the sex doll, represents a real threat to the trade of human sex workers. Ryann Connell reported on this growing trend in a 2005 article in the *Mainichi Daily News:* "Rent-a-Doll Blows Hooker Market Wide Open."

> Several companies are involved in the bustling trade sup-
> plying customers looking to slip it into some silicon[e],
> with lifelike figurines that set back buyers something in
> the vicinity of 600,000 yen (almost $5,000), as opposed
> to the simple blow-up types with the permanently open
> mouths that can be bought from vending machines for a
> few thousand yen. Prime among the sellers of silicon[e]
> sex workers is *Doll no Mori,* which runs a 24-hour service
> supplying love dolls, or "Dutch wives" as the Japanese call
> them, to customers in southern Tokyo and neighboring
> Kanagawa Prefecture.
>
> "We opened for business in July this year," said Ha-
> jime Kimura, owner of *Doll no Mori.* "Originally, we
> were going to run a regular call girl service, but one day
> while we were surfing the Net we found this business
> offering love doll deliveries. We decided the labor costs
> would be cheaper and changed our line of business."
>
> Outlays are low, with the doll's initial cost the major
> investment and wages never a problem for employers.
> "We've got four dolls working for us at the moment. We
> get at least one job a day, even on weekdays, so we made
> back our initial investment in the first month," Kimura
> says. "Unlike employing people, everything we make
> becomes a profit and we never have to worry about the
> girls not turning up for work."
>
> *Doll no Mori* charges start at 13,000 yen (around
> $110) for a 70-minute session with the dolls, which is

about the same price as a regular call girl service. The
company boasts of many repeat customers and a membership clientele topping 200. "Nearly all our customers
choose our two-hour option."

Within little more than a year after the doll-for-hire idea took root
in Japan, sex entrepreneurs in South Korea also started to cash in.
Upmarket sex dolls were introduced to the Korean public at the
Sexpo exhibition, held in the Seoul Trade Exhibition Center in
August 2005. They were seen as a possible antidote to Korea's Special Law on Prostitution that had been placed on the statute books
in 2004, and before long, Korean hotels were hiring out "doll experience rooms" for around 25,000 won per hour (around $25), a
fee that included a bed, a computer to enable the customer to visit
pornographic sites, and the use of a doll. This initiative quickly became so successful at plugging the gap created by the antiprostitu-
tion law that soon some establishments opened that were devoted
solely to the use of sex dolls, including at least four in the city of
Suwon. The owners of these hotels assumed, quite reasonably, that
there was no question of their running foul of the law, since the
dolls were not human. But the Korean police were not so sure.
The news website Chosun.com reported, in October 2006, that the
police in Gyeonggi province had confirmed that they were "looking into whether these businesses violate the law...Since the sex
acts are occurring with a doll and not a human being, it is unclear
whether the Special Law on Prostitution applies."

Although the idea of hiring out these dolls appears to be attracting interest from entrepreneurs, the sex-doll industry is still
in its infancy and still very much catering to the desires of men, as
demonstrated by the fact that of the fifteen models offered on the
RealDoll website, fourteen are made in the likeness of women and

intended for sale to men, while only one is modeled on a man. A likely reason for this disparity—though not the only reason, I'm sure—is that RealDoll's Charlie typically sells for $7,000, and there are far fewer women than men who have thousands of dollars of readily disposable income. But an alternative explanation that has been put forward for the disparity is one with which I strongly disagree—the suggestion that far fewer women than men are interested in using artificial means for getting some or all of their sexual stimulation and for achieving orgasm. Many women claim that the use of sex dolls is very much a "guy thing," but surely such a claim is easily refuted by the widespread use of vibrators among modern women.

NOTES:

1. A comprehensive line of sex dolls and other sex machines is shown, for example, on www.fuckingmachines.com.

2. CyberSkin is a natural-feeling material that mimics human flesh. It is formed by combining silicone and latex.

3. The branch of medicine dealing with the reproductive and excretory organs.

4. December 11, 2003.

5. *Dacapo* is a Japanese news digest with a focus on current event feature stories.

6. April 21, 2004.

7. The most authoritative explanation for the origin of the term "Dutch wives" is found in Alan Pate's 2005 book *Ningyo: The Art of the Japanese Doll*. They were originally leather dolls carried aboard Dutch merchant ships, beginning in the seventeenth century; and through their interaction with the Dutch on the trade island of Deshima, established by the Dutch East India company in 1641, the Japanese became familiar with the practice. Pate's own source for this origin was Mitamura Engyo's book *Takeda Hachidai—Eight Generations of the Takeda Family*.

Dear John
Susannah Breslin

As a journalist I've covered the sex beat for over a decade. I've interviewed call girls and johns, adult film stars and dominatrices, strippers and pimps. I've seen a side of America that most Americans don't see. In the movies there are heart-of-gold hookers like Julia Roberts in *Pretty Woman,* falling in love with a john who happens to be a sensitive guy capable of overlooking her profession. But in reality we don't know much about johns or the complicated reasons they pay for sex. So when New York Governor Eliot Spitzer, a zealous former prosecutor of prostitution rings, was accused of using one himself, many people questioned how such a smart man could have put his family and his career on the line.

A research project I'm working on may yield some answers to that perplexing question. Earlier this year I posted an online call for letters from johns, asking men to send me anonymous letters about their experiences soliciting sex. In most cases the johns came

144

across Letters from Johns while surfing the Internet. I'd considered soliciting johns from sites like Craigslist, but I decided to let them seek me out. Most of the letters, I believe, are real; in some cases the men sent them from their personal email accounts, signed their real names, and included links to their professional websites. The fake letters are for the most part easy to identify; they lack detail—and frequently end with scenes in which the sex worker returns the money because the sex was so good.

Thus far I've received letters from nearly two dozen johns about why they did it. The men come from all walks of life, ranging in age and across socioeconomic classes. In many cases, like Spitzer, they're married. Many report they are in relationships with women who are no longer interested in sex. Some of the men are in long-term relationships; some are single. Some seek out streetwalkers, while others solicit high-end escorts as Spitzer is alleged to have done. The men find the women in bars, on Craigslist, in adult ads in the backs of their local weeklies.

Often these guys aren't just looking for sex. Many are depressed or stressed, lonely or bored, looking for intimacy or a connection, no matter how transient, no matter the cost. One john who was rejected on a regular basis in the dating scene wrote that, in contrast to the women he met at bars, prostitutes saw him as "a normal and charming guy." Other men recalled youthful sexcapades in the military while deployed overseas, from a German brothel called Crazy Sexy to a barbershop in Asia where women performed oral sex on men getting haircuts. An "overeducated" twenty-eight-year-old went through a bad breakup, a death in the family, and the loss of his job. Online he found a "courtesan" who taught him what he wanted in a relationship and gave him his confidence back. "I'm really grateful to her," he reported.

One letter in particular may offer a window into the mind-set of a man like Spitzer. It came in the form of an encrypted email from a state investigator. Professionally, he was dedicated to enforcing the law. Personally, he was in a relationship with a woman with whom he hadn't had sex in years. He'd been seeing prostitutes since 1991. In his encoded diary he recorded his encounters. "1 dot is oral, 2 dots is vaginal sex, and 2 connected dots is anal sex. In the event that someone questions the dots, they are associated with good or bad days: no dots are normal days, 1 dot is a good day, 2 dots is a great day, and 2 connected dots is the best day for that week." For him, sex for money was sex without strings, attachment, or guilt—a transaction.

But for some it's the financial transaction itself that is alluring. In the first letter I received I heard from a successful twentysomething who described himself as "attractive and ambitious." He had a girl-friend—"a wonderful woman"—but there was something about the act of paying for sex, he confessed, that turned him on. "I find the idea of paying for sexual acts to be erotic," he confided. For some men, especially those who are seen as particularly moral or righteous in their public lives (think of all those fallen preachers), part of the appeal is the fact that it is illegal and a moral transgression in their eyes.

What do the women think about why men come to them? As a companion project to Letters from Johns, I created Letters from Working Girls. While johns are eager to confess, letters from working girls are few and far between. But one high-end call girl I spoke to about the Spitzer affair said there are lots of reasons a man in such a prominent position might seek high-stakes sex with a prostitute. Why not just have an affair, which probably wouldn't have destroyed his career? She said that Spitzer, if he did use prostitutes, was probably one of those men for whom the payoff was the excitement of doing something really taboo. "What could be more taboo than going to an agency when you're a crusader for all that is moral and good?" she theorized. "It's only natural," this call girl asserted, "that they'd hire a girl to get off." She speculates that there was probably a "midlife crisis element" there too.

Of course, Spitzer was no ordinary middle-aged shlub. Agencies like the Emperors Club screen workers and clients alike, and discretion was part of what he'd have been paying for. Followers of Spitzergate have speculated as to what Client 9's date, Kristen, knew when the club's booker said that her famous client, who had been described by other girls as a "difficult" customer, "would ask you to do things that, like, you might not think were safe." The wording might imply something kinky, but it's more likely that Client 9 was attempting to get Kristen to have sex without a condom—a common and unwelcome request, according to many sex workers. As one self-described twentysomething redhead I heard from (who solicited men on Craigslist to pay off her college loans) asked rhetorically, "How can someone even consider not using a condom with a woman who does it for a living?" That added risk factor may heighten the sexual excitement. For some guys the lure of that particular thrill can obscure any worries about long-term repercussions.

Over these last months I have seen one common thread in the johns' stories: many remain conflicted about paying for sex. Was it right? Was it wrong? Is there more going on than just a need for sex? With his career a shambles, Spitzer may soon have more time than he'd like to contemplate those very questions.

Oldest Profession 2.0: A New Generation of Local "Providers" and "Hobbyists" Create a Virtual Red-Light District

Keegan Hamilton

If you're researching auto repair on the Internet and stumble across www.stlasp.com, you might well hit your web browser's back button before noticing anything amiss.

Read on, though, and you'll raise an eyebrow. "This site is for entertainment purposes only. It is a place where users can post fantasies or stories for other members to view...The information on this site is intended for adult audiences only, by definition, in the state of Missouri, you must be 18 or older to view the information on this site...."

These folks must really love their cars!

Beyond the homepage, it quickly becomes evident that "STLASP" stands for "St. Louis Adult Service Providers"—an entirely different kind of body work. Here the "providers" are prostitutes—or, if you like your euphemisms, escorts—and their customers are "hobbyists." STLASP is the virtual forum in which they discuss everything from gardening to philosophy to how they prefer one another's pubic hair to be groomed. They alert each other to possible police stings and scam artists in the "Erotic Services" section of Craigslist. And customers—seemingly all of them men—write and post lengthy reviews of their experiences with the call girls.

An escort herself, the site's creator says she founded STLASP in June of last year after moving to the St. Louis area from Southern California, where she'd been involved in a nearly identical online community. She found that the message board not only made her job safer by allowing her to screen her clients, it also created a tight-knit network of the region's online escorts, providing a forum for them to share knowledge, including concerns about potentially dangerous johns.

"I'm trying to educate the women and give them a chance to feel safe and feel a connection with others that are in the same industry," says the woman, who agreed to be interviewed for this story on the condition that she not reveal her real name and that she be referred to as "Mac."

"There's a lot of power in numbers. I'm trying to educate them to be as independent as they can and make smart choices."

The idea of escorts on the Internet is nothing new—the oldest profession has long embraced twenty-first-century technology. But according to Stacey Swimme, cofounder of sex worker–rights organizations the Desiree Alliance and the Sex Workers Outreach Project (SWOP) Mac's site is part of an emerging national trend: prostitutes have turned to the Internet and small, independently operated message boards as a means of empowerment.

"From what I've been researching about the sex industry over the past twenty-five years, that is the biggest change," Swimme says. "Providers are talking to each other. That is a force to be reckoned with. That is where political power comes from, is that sort of community-building."

STLASP's "Reviews" section contains more than seven thousand posts. Many are based on a review template in which "hobbyists" share their experiences with local providers.

Examples:

Did the ASP's photos accurately portray her?
Was she punctual?
Did she pressure you into tipping?
And, of course: Activities between consenting adults (what did you do)?

The reviews are peppered with abbreviations and jargon. An escort might be a "FOTC" (fuck of the century) or a DFE ("dead fish experience"). When johns say "CMD" (carpet matches drapes) or "Hardwood Floors," they're referring to their date's body hair, not her taste in interior decorating.

While phrases like "She spoke French without an interpreter" and "We took a trip to the Mediterranean" carry one meaning in a newspaper travel section, on STLASP they refer to oral sex without a condom and anal sex, respectively.

Reviewers may wax passionate: "I would advise you to take your vitamins, drink lots of fluids, eat your Wheaties, and get plenty of rest before your date," one recently wrote. "She will wear you out."

Or merely state the obvious: "The massage is not therapeutic, not a professional style, muscle-relaxing type massage. But if you enjoy a very pretty girl spreading lotion all over your body, you will be pleased."

The practice of posting online reviews of escorts dates back about ten years. David Elms, creator of the Erotic Review (www. theeroticreview.com), claims his website was one of the first to encourage men to provide feedback about their clandestine encounters. Reached by phone in his Southern California office, Elms explains that he got the idea after being ripped off by a call girl.

"It was a way that people could be held accountable for their actions in this industry," Elms says. "Now girls prefer that they find clients on the Erotic Review. It already tells a guy all the juicy details, so he doesn't have to ask stupid questions."

Elms says his website, created in 1999, now attracts more than 300,000 visitors a day, and that half of the site's users log on more than once a day. He collects information about each person who registers an account and says the average hobbyist is between thirty-five and fifty-five years old with a median income of eighty thousand dollars.

From the sex worker–rights perspective, Swimme has no qualms about the commodification that is taking place. She suggests that the practice of posting reviews adds legitimacy to an otherwise illicit transaction. "I think that having reviews in the sex industry to some degree makes a lot of sense," she says. "It brings it into a realm that says: this is a commercial exchange, a profession, a service."

Elms goes as far as to compare the john-escort dynamic to the purchase of expensive electronics: "It's like a consumer-reports magazine that has buyer reviews of car-stereo performance."

The quest for rave reviews and the booming business that comes with them can be hypercompetitive. One of the oldest and most popular review websites, bigdoggie.net, issues a twice-daily top-100 ranking of escorts from across the nation based on ratings tallied from user reviews.

The practice does have its critics. Amanda Brooks, author of *The Internet Escort's Handbook,* a three-part series first published in 2006 that professes to "address every question that a woman could ask before she becomes a sex worker who advertises through the Internet," points out that women can be pressured into doing things they otherwise wouldn't do, for fear of the online backlash.

"It has turned into, 'This girl is totally great, she's going to do this and this and this,'" says Brooks, who also contributes to Bound, Not Gagged, a sex worker–rights blog. "That's a big problem, because girls will do sex activities that push boundaries, but they do them because they could get a good review and make money."

At STLASP, Mac says when she first got into the business, the creator of one review site pressured her to have sex with him in exchange for positive reviews. "He said he could make me or break me because his site was national, and if I was smart I would come visit him and have an appointment with him for free," she recalls. "I told him no way."

Despite that experience, Mac remains a strong advocate of posting the critiques "for the sake of quality control." She admits, however, to having to frequently mediate disputes about authenticity and accuracy. Several times women have been caught creating fake profiles in order to post positive evaluations of themselves. Once, Mac says, a man posted a negative review that an escort later claimed was completely off base.

"I told her that she could write a rebuttal to the review and she chose not to," Mac notes.

Elms says he has confronted similar issues. "I look at the history of the reviewer," he says. "If, consistently, this reviewer's history shows he's been accurate, no one has ever contested anything, and he has long-term membership, then I know that this is probably pretty solid."

Then again, Elms adds, reviews are rarely two thumbs down. "When you tell a story to a couple of friends, obviously you're going to put yourself in a good light," he notes. "When you tell a story here, you're telling it to 100,000 of your closest friends. You still have the male ego to deal with."

When Mac debuted STLASP a year ago, she promoted it with a mere two posts on Craigslist. Since then an average of fifty new people per day have registered for user names. A counter at the bottom of the site's main page tallies the current membership at nearly 2,500; altogether they account for more than 19,000 posts.

Registration is free, and all that is required to access the forums is an email address, a user name, and a password. Fearing the site has began to attract too much attention, Mac recently posted a message saying she is considering a moratorium on new memberships.

For a site that specializes in sex, STLASP's appearance is remarkably sterile: blue text on a plain gray-and-white background. The site is divided into several sections, each of which contains its own message boards. "Administration" features a glossary of "hobby"-related abbreviations. In "Providers" users can see which women are "Available Today" and browse the personal web pages of two dozen escorts. Most of the posts are found in the "Hobbyists" section, which features the "Discussion" board, where the men and women tell jokes, swap stories, and ask each other questions about nearly everything under the sun.

Unlike other sites of its kind, STLASP is devoid of advertisements. Mac says she has invested several hundred dollars in software, server space, and the domain name. She estimates that she generally spends multiple hours each week dealing with programming glitches, creating new features, and moderating disputes between users. Having had no prior web-design experience, she concedes she may have gotten in over her head with her not-for-profit endeavor.

"This does not define who I am as a person," Mac says. "It's a very small aspect of my life. The more I invest time into it, the more it becomes a bigger part of my life. And since I've been spending like five hours a night on this website, I'm like, 'Oh, my God, it's taking over now.' "

Swimme is impressed that the mind behind STLASP is a woman's.

"I love to see when it's actually service providers who are out founding these sites," Stacey Swimme says. "It's much more common for hobbyists to create these communities. As an advocate, I'm always thrilled to support the work of individual sex workers who pioneer their own free-speech spaces."

In the world of STLASP, however, "free speech" is a relative term. One of Mac's earliest posts under her "Admin" handle is a lengthy "code of ethics" that lays out rules for maintaining civil discourse. "Do unto others, as you would have them do to you," she writes. "Do not post against somebody in a rude or nasty manner...We all have a different perspective on life and general topics so respect others and they will respect you."

The software for the forums automatically censors some content. Try to type the words "sex" or "money" into a post and they're instantly altered to "sensual fun" and "donation."

Such safeguards don't bar the site's users from self-indulgence. Women post pictures of themselves, often blurring their faces (but not much else) in hopes of concealing their identity. Men ask which local strip clubs offer "full service" and tip each other off to "UTR" (under the radar) adult establishments, such as a salon in a St. Louis suburb that offers a haircut with a happy ending. They frequently poke fun at their "Auto Specialists" pretext with threads like: "Pole position—how do you prefer to start the race."

Some exchanges border on the cerebral. Observes one user in a February post on a lengthy thread entitled "Morality, Ethics, and the Hobby": "Our Western society's anti-sensuality attitude foundations were laid around 430 CE with the philosophy of St. Augustine. It can be traced further back to the Gnostic Christians rejection of the physical world and the body as well as some of the letters of St. Paul."

"My personnel [*sic*] morals and code of ethics calls to treat everyone with respect and human dignity in all my interpersonal encounters," reads one of the replies. "For hobbyists it means being a gentleman with providers and treating them with the utmost respect a gentlemen [*sic*] gives a lady. For providers it means not treating the hobbyist as just another envelope but as a fellow human being that wants to do what comes naturally."

In another thread begun in March, a poster writes, "The way I see it, indulging in this hobby is wrong. But I still do it because there is pleasure involved. I just haven't been able to cheat my inner moral compass into believing that it is OK," concluding in all-boldface, "It's wrong. Still, I do it."

In an email in which he declined to be interviewed for this story, STLASP's moderator, a user Mac deputized to police the forums for spam and other prohibited content who posts under the handle "luvs2duit," described the STLASP community.

"There are a lot of very good people in here," he writes. "The fact that they hobby doesn't mean that they love their SOs [significant others] any less, or meet their obligations to the community any less, or are blatant in their choice of lifestyle."

He then requested that *Riverfront Times* not pursue a story about STLASP:

"Our happy little life may be seriously damaged because folks outside the community will still view us as cheaters and perverts that violate the social norms. The fact is, many of us are much happier than our repressed neighbors."

A sandy blonde in her thirties, Mac says she has been an escort for the past three years. She says that in addition to working on a graduate degree at an area university, she is her family's main bread-winner. Fearing it would jeopardize her anonymity, she declined a request to provide documents to support her purported résumé.

Before moving to Missouri, Mac says, she lived and attended college in Southern California. A single mom at the time, she be-gan working as a stripper to make ends meet. Eventually, she says, she began commuting to Las Vegas on the weekends to work at the city's lucrative strip clubs. When she suffered a knee injury and could no longer dance, she became an escort.

She says the decision was as easy as clicking a mouse: she placed an ad in the "Erotic Services" section of Craigslist.

Mac had little trouble emotionally adjusting to her new lifestyle. "Actually it was kind of exciting for me," she says sheepishly. "I know that sounds funny, but it was actually exciting. It turned me on. I liked it. I was like: 'Wow, this is something really hot.'"

She is emphatic that she became an escort of her own volition, that she has never had a pimp, and that she doesn't touch drugs. (During an interview at a west-county bar that lasted several hours, she didn't order a drink.)

She says she specializes in "GFE," commonly employed short-hand for "girlfriend experience." The term is loosely defined, but Mac describes it as doing anything the "ideal companion" would. Needless to say, that includes the intimate act frowned upon in *Pretty Woman:* kissing on the mouth. (Two GFE-related entries from the "Abbreviations" glossary: DFK = Deep French Kissing; LFK = Light Face Kissing.) It also means, Mac says, being excited to see her date, appearing to be genuinely interested in what they have to say, and not rushing to leave.

For her services, Mac charges anywhere from $350 an hour to several thousand dollars for a weekend or multiple-hour stay.

"I'm like a therapist," she explains. "Sometimes I'm a mom, sometimes I'm a wife, sometimes a slut, sometimes I'm a girlfriend, a sister. Sometimes people just need someone to care. So many people are just unloved. There are times when I have an appointment when I feel so good because I feel like I've been able to touch somebody emotionally that maybe hasn't been touched in a long time."

Asked directly whether she enjoys what she does for a living, she responds, "I think that I do like what I do most days. I make the schedule, I work when I want to work, and I don't when I don't. I choose to do my job, I don't have to. That's a big deal in this industry.

"If you're not sound emotionally, this industry will tear you down," she adds. "There are definitely days where it's maybe not a good day, where I feel like it's affected me more. But those are few and far between. If I'm having a bad day, it's not a good day to be working. I think for some ladies, that can be a pitfall."

Mac says her spouse knows about her profession and approves of it. But, she adds, "My biggest fear is always my kids finding out. Everything else is just things that I can take care of. But that will never leave my child if they ever found out. I could never take that back."

Stacey Swimme says many women use Craigslist as a jumping-off point into prostitution. The anonymity the site affords users, coupled with the fact that it's free, popular, and easy to use, render it about as close as America currently comes to the decriminalization of sex work.

"I think of Craigslist as training wheels," says Swimme. "When a girl wants to work in the sex industry, she ought to able to contact a local union and ask, 'What kind of materials do I need? What training do I need?' Since that's not available, Craigslist is the easiest way."

It was the lack of resources for women starting out in the field that spurred Amanda Brooks, a Dallas-based former call girl, to author her *Internet Escort's Handbook.*

"Craigslist is generally people who haven't really studied the business, so they end up taking a lot of risks," Brooks says when reached by phone. "Often they don't screen [their customers], which is very unsafe, and the men who surf Craigslist generally aren't your better clients. And police have been busting girls on there ever since it started."

"I didn't screen my clients at first," Mac says of her early Craigslist experience. "I was really naive, I didn't know how to really protect myself. I didn't know about a lot of message boards [like STLASP]. I didn't know any of this, so I was taking a big risk." Now she requires potential clients to fill out an online form that includes home and work phone numbers—which she calls to verify their identities.

One of STLASP's most popular forums is devoted exclusively to discussing Craigslist's "Erotic Services" pages. Hundreds of posts come from users asking their peers to verify that a particular ad isn't a fake or a police sting. Another forum, "Alerts," is devoted to pointing out "Robs"—escorts who show up intending to blackmail a client.

"I take all posts [on Craigslist] with a grain of salt," one user recently wrote. "There is so much drama and cut throat [*sic*] practices on there that almost everything on it is BS."

Mac says she has gone out of her way to enforce standards to make her site different from Craigslist. Anyone who types in all-caps, can't spell properly, or relies too much on web shorthand—all trademarks of the red-light section of the San Francisco-based classifieds site—is banned. (One of the longest-running threads on STLASP is devoted to the unintentionally hilarious misspellings and mistakes that appear on Craigslist. (Two highlights:

"I'm available all mourning" and "Super Bowel specials.")

As Craigslist, chatrooms, and social-networking sites have skyrocketed in popularity, they've increasingly become the focus of academic research. Social scientists have begun to study how the anonymity afforded by the medium affects human behavior. Not surprisingly, some researchers have examined online communities that focus on sex.

In a paper called "The Gender Dynamics of Online Sex Talk," presented last year at the European Gender and Internet Communication Technology Symposium at the University of Helsinki, Chrystie Myketiak writes that "[s]ocial expectations and norms work to keep sexuality and sexual topics that, though culturally ubiquitous, are considered bad taste to openly discuss. On the Internet, people face fewer consequences for deviating from dominant social norms and can explore topics in ways that seem confidential and anonymous."

Myketiak, who is working toward a PhD at Queen Mary University of London, reached her findings via "a qualitative analysis of more than two years of conversational [chat] logs" on an Internet forum.

Members of forums like STLASP have begun to shed the veil of anonymity the Internet provides. Many sites, STLASP included, host "meet and greets" where prominent personalities on the board gather at a local pub to match faces with screen names.

"It's so odd that escorts and clients are talking and having socials," says *Internet Escort's Handbook* author Brooks. "That has no historical precedent. Honestly, it's a new thing the Internet has spawned—and there's nothing wrong with it."

A thread on STLASP is devoted to a recent "happy hour" gathering at Flamingo Bowl downtown. The group reserved lanes under their "auto specialists" guise.

"The great thing about an event like this is that you get to talk to folks and learn so much more than we do online," moderator "luvs2duit" wrote afterward. "The ladies get a chance to place a face and personality with the screen names and posts they have seen online. These events are a wonderful chance to break the ice."

A user observed that many of the working women in attendance didn't look much like mechanics:

"It was fun watching the non-associated males in the place and the ones walking on the street outside get whiplash from their double takes."

Not all online escort reviews are as prim and proper as STLASP. One site, usasexguide.info, features reviews of streetwalkers. There are forums devoted exclusively to "the strolls" of Brooklyn and Washington Park, Illinois, whose posts are littered with references to drugs, pimps, and abuse.

On STLASP, in a January thread titled "How many providers did you see in 2007," most members said they stuck with "professional providers"—including one man who estimated that he spent $13,000 on his "hobby." Still, several users wrote that they frequently picked up women on the street.

For Mac, it's a troubling reality that she says she wants to avoid. "I don't even want to entertain the idea of reviewing streetwalkers," she says. "It's a whole different industry that I know nothing about. There's been a lot of gripes from other ladies on the board saying they don't want it either.

"I don't want to make any negative remarks toward these women," she hastens to add. "In fact, I have a lot of compassion for them. But the risks that they take are so huge that it's scary to me."

Of course, risk isn't limited to street hookers. In addition to sexually transmitted disease, the threat of local law enforcement looms for online operators.

"Escort services, whether online or not, are basically prostitution," asserts Assistant United States Attorney Howard Marcus, who is based in St. Louis. "Most of the women that end up working in this area are all, despite what they might say, victims. It takes a toll on your life, it takes a toll on your family life. Many have a history of alcoholism, drug abuse, and domestic problems. There's typically a traumatic event, some kind of abuse, that leads them into this line of work."

Marcus says the most common charges stemming from investigations of online escort rings are money laundering and, because many sites are hosted on servers located in another state, the use of interstate facilities to promote prostitution. The latter crime carries a minimum five-year sentence and a $250,000 fine.

One St. Louis-area municipality, Maryland Heights, has gained a reputation for its tough stance on online prostitution. STLASP users report that the city frequently conducts stings on Craigslist and backpage.com.

"I don't like to see anyone [provider or hobbyist] get popped," one poster wrote last month. "But if a person is dumb enough to work out of/make an appointment in MH…it serves them right IMHO."

A spokesman for the Maryland Heights police department did not return calls seeking comment for this story.

The STLASP community takes several precautions when it comes to dealing with law enforcement. Most women require at least two "references" from fellow escorts before seeing a new customer. Some ask their clientele to use the online identity-verification services at date-check.com or preferred411.com.

Mac looks forward to the day prostitution law is reformed and references become aboveboard. "I think that there should be some regulations," she allows. "But I do think that it should be legal. I think that people should have to get a license to do it. I think that they should have regulations on health checkups and have certain guidelines so people are safe and healthy and make sure that they are not working on the street."

In the meantime, Swimme, who once marched topless around San Francisco's federal building in protest of then-Attorney General John Ashcroft's strict policies on prostitution, says women will increasingly turn to sites like STLASP as a means of protecting themselves:

"As long as prostitution is illegal, people will be dependent on these types of forums to stay safe."

Mac agrees. She and others on STLASP keep a blacklist of men who have hygiene problems or who they feel might be dangerous. One of the features on the site she's most proud of is the "Ladies Only" forum.

"We have what we call the 'woman to woman,' " Mac explains. "We talk amongst ourselves about any topic—it could be about the business or not. We're just helping each other out. If we can stay together and inform each other, there's a lot of power in that. It's like social capital.

"To me, that's what this is: we're building social capital."

How "Swingers" Might Save Hollywood from a Federal Pornography Statute
Alan Levy

Section 2257 of title 18 of the U.S. Code requires that "producers" of photographs and films of "actual sexually explicit conduct" create and maintain records documenting the age of the performers depicted in those performances. The statute's purpose is to ensure that the performers are not minors. This recordkeeping statute has generally been limited to the adult film industry, although recently the statute's impact has crept into the realm of mainstream film and television. For over two decades, the statute has withstood numerous constitutional challenges by the adult film industry and civil libertarian organizations. On October 23, 2007, however, the U.S. Court of Appeals for the Sixth Circuit held that § 2257 was overbroad on its face and therefore unconstitutional.

Although the Sixth Circuit has since vacated the *Connection III* decision to rehear the case en banc, this decision marks the first time that a federal appeals court has struck down the recordkeeping statute on constitutional grounds. Ironically, the victorious plaintiff was not the adult film industry or a civil liberties organization but rather a noncommercial "swingers" publication in which married couples published explicit photographs of themselves to seek out other married couples for sexual relationships. While the court protected the constitutional rights of swingers, this decision will also impact the speech rights of both the adult film industry and the mainstream entertainment industry. Even though the full Sixth Circuit decision will replace that of the appellate panel, the reasoning in the earlier decision will lay out the framework for the arguments in this case and future challenges to the statute.

The Birth of 18 U.S.C. § 2257

In 1986, the Meese Commission issued its final report following its investigation into the impact of pornography. At that time, there was significant media attention and controversy involving "Traci Lords," a woman who performed in dozens of adult films despite being under the age of eighteen. Two years later, Congress enacted the Child Protection and Obscenity Enforcement Act of 1988, creating § 2257 of title 18 of the U.S. Code which authorized the Attorney General to promulgate regulations requiring producers of sexually explicit materials to maintain records ensuring that all adult entertainment performers were, in fact, adults.

In the nearly twenty years since the passage of the statute, § 2257 has endured numerous court challenges, both questioning the constitutionality of the statute itself and the validity of the Attorney General's regulations. In 1995, one aspect of these regulations became especially controversial. Not only were "primary" producers required to maintain records attesting to the age and identity of the performers, but "secondary" producers (that is, anyone who "publishes, reproduces, or reissues" explicit material) were also obligated to maintain such records even if they had no contact with the performers. Furthermore, § 2257 authorizes federal agents to conduct inspections of these records without advanced notice. The regulations as they applied to "secondary" producers were struck down by the Tenth Circuit.

In 2003, Congress amended § 2257 to expand the definition of the term "produces" to include creation of a "computer generated image, digital image, or picture." Following this amendment, the Attorney General updated federal regulations, again requiring "secondary" producers to maintain records of performers. This rule caused a great deal of concern throughout the Internet, since anyone who posts a sexually explicit image on a website would need to maintain records of the performers, even though he or she would invariably have no contact with the performers.

These updated regulations concerning "secondary" producers were nearly identical to the regulations that the Tenth Circuit struck down in *Sundance*. Later that year, a federal district court issued a preliminary injunction enjoining the government from enforcing the new regulations. Congress, in an apparent attempt to enshrine the twice-invalidated regulations, enacted the Adam Walsh Child Protection and Safety Act of 2006, which added many of the definitions of "secondary" producers to the statute itself.

The Government Expands the Recordkeeping Requirement to Hollywood: The Birth of § 2257A

The passage of the Adam Walsh Child Protection and Safety Act of 2006 also created § 2257A of title 18 of the U.S. Code. Section 2257A requires producers of "simulated sexually explicit conduct" to create and maintain records relating to the age of performers. Unlike § 2257, which defines "actual sexually explicit conduct," § 2257A never lays out a definition of "simulated sexually explicit conduct." This law could thus potentially encompass any Hollywood film that includes a lovemaking scene.

Mainstream filmmakers should be especially concerned with the language of the most recent published § 2257 regulations, in which Attorney General Alberto Gonzales wrote, "Section 2257A requires that producers of visual depictions of simulated sexually explicit conduct maintain records documenting that performers in those depictions not be minors." Does this mean that a noted film such as *Taxi Driver*, in which a twelve-year-old Jodie Foster portrays a thirteen-year-old prostitute, is unlawful? What about the more recent controversial film *Hounddog*, which premiered at the 2007 Sundance Film Festival and portrayed twelve-year-old Dakota Fanning as a rape victim? Even a film nominated for Best Picture at the 2008 Academy Awards may be affected by § 2257A. *Atonement* has one scene of explicit simulated sexual conduct involving actress Juno Temple, who was seventeen years of age at the time of filming.

Recently, more mainstream filmmakers have been portraying scenes of actual sexual explicit conduct in their films. As a result, even though these works could not be reasonably characterized as pornographic adult films, they are nonetheless under the scope of § 2257.

The Sixth Circuit's Decision

Connection III was the culmination of twelve years of litigation that had traveled up and down the federal court system. The case began in 1995 when Connection, a publisher of "swingers" magazines, filed suit challenging the constitutionality of § 2257. Along with articles and editorials relating to the "swinging" lifestyle, Connection's magazine would also include member-submitted sexually explicit photographs of couples seeking to meet other couples.

The court held that the 2006 amendments to § 2257 significantly expanded what materials are impacted by the statute. Specifically, the statute covered all sexually explicit photographs and images regardless of whether they were produced for commercial purposes or with the intent to be shown to others. Consequently, "a married couple who videotape or photograph themselves in the bedroom engaging in sexually explicit conduct would be required to keep records, affix disclosure statements to the images, and hold their home open to government agents for records inspections."

While the court did not dispute the legitimacy of the government's goal of eradicating child pornography, it noted that this regulation of protected legal speech does not further that aim. There already exists a statutory regime that makes the production and distribution of child pornography illegal. In that regard, the court held that the § 2257 is overbroad and infringes on constitutionally protected speech.

In holding that the statute was overbroad, the court identified two constitutional rights that were being infringed. First, adults have the constitutional right to engage in sexual conduct. Second, individuals have the right to engage in anonymous speech—a right violated by § 2257's requirement that individuals reveal their real names.

The court further warned that statutes are especially suspect when "enforcers can seek out and silence particularly disliked people or speech." The court appeared to frame "swingers" as such a group deserving of constitutional protection. Finally, the court identified the chilling effect of § 2257:

> Assume a couple wishes to take photographs of themselves engaging in sexual activity. To do so means compiling records, affixing statements, maintaining such

records for at least five years, and opening their property up for visitation by government officials to inspect the records. It seems unlikely the couple would choose to speak when faced with such requirements, which if violated means being guilty of a felony punishable by up to five years in prison plus fines.

The court also identified another fatal flaw in the statute: producers were required to maintain records for all performers, even if they were unmistakably of legal age. The court feared that the statute burdened speech that in no way resembled child pornography. Indeed, married couples in their fifties or sixties who take photographs of themselves engaging in sexually explicit conduct would be subject to severe criminal penalties if they failed to maintain the proper records. Advocates for the adult film industry often cite the examples of noted adult stars Nina Hartley and Ron Jeremy, who must comply with § 2257 despite having performed on-screen for over twenty years. This begs the question of how requiring middle-aged performers to maintain such records fulfills the government purpose of fighting child pornography. Clearly, the Sixth Circuit was also troubled by this question in holding that the statute was impermissibly broad in chilling this protected form of speech.

The Impact of *Connection III*

The repercussions of *Connection III* are unclear, and the only certainty is that there will be a *Connection IV*. The next several months will be crucial in determining the future of § 2257 and its younger sibling, § 2257A. Nevertheless, *Connection III* will likely benefit not only the adult film industry, but also Hollywood. As written, these statutes may give great concern to all filmmakers and artists. Will a director choose to cut an erotic scene from his or her film because of artistic reasons or because of legal concerns? Will a casting director refuse to hire a minor actor because the scene involves simulated sexuality? Judging from *Connection III*, this type of chilling effect will generate heightened judicial scrutiny.

Furthermore, it is interesting to note that § 2257A also permits producers to forego maintaining records of each performance so long as they certify to the Attorney General that they regularly and in the course of normal business collect and maintain such records for tax purposes pursuant to the industry standards. Clearly, this "opt-out" clause was created to provide added protection to Hollywood studios. The opt-out clause in § 2257A may relieve Hollywood producers from much of the overly burdensome paperwork requirements of § 2257, but the question of whether it is unlawful to cast an underage actress for scenes of simulated sexuality remains unanswered.

Section 2257A's opt-out provision may create another problem, since it creates a scenario whereby two protected forms of speech are being regulated differently. In the case of actual explicit content, each performer must maintain separate records for each performance and cannot opt out. Meanwhile, simulated content can opt out of this requirement merely by submitting a certification to the Attorney General. This difference makes it difficult for the government to assert that the regulations are content-neutral. A future challenge to either of the statutes could easily ask the court to apply a heightened strict scrutiny standard. By passing § 2257A into law, Congress may have given more reason for the courts to invalidate the entire statutory scheme.

While the government is pursuing appellate remedies, Congress could amend the statute to help it pass constitutional muster. The last major amendment to the statute, however, was passed in the closing months of a Republican-controlled Congress. Since the Democratic takeover of Congress, there does not appear to be much political drive to amend the statute in the near future. Depending on the outcome of the *Connection* matter and the results of the 2008 election, though, § 2257 may once again be amended to remedy its constitutional flaws.

•

Why Bathroom Sex Is Hot
James Hannaham

When Idaho Senator Larry Craig says, "I'm not gay," I believe him. But that doesn't mean he wasn't cruising for sex last June when he was arrested in a bathroom at the Minneapolis-St. Paul Airport on charges of disorderly conduct. Surely any homosexual worth his capri pants saw the loopholes in Craig's televised declaration of nongayness, amplified by the presence of his wife. Even some straight folks, wised up after the scandals of Ted Haggard and Mark Foley, must have noted that Craig did not add a qualifying phrase like, "Nor am I bisexual," "I've never had sex with a man," or even one of those oldies but goodies like, "Doing what I did doesn't make you gay," "I was so drunk!," or "I'm only queer for some guys."

As Haggard and Foley could perhaps have told Craig, bathroom stalls may be tight quarters, but the closet is big enough to fit plenty of religious, conservative Republicans. (In fact, they seem to be crowding everyone else out lately.) What no straight Republican man has the balls to explain—no matter how much Democratic gay sex he's had—is the eternal appeal of cottaging.

"Cottaging" is the British term for soliciting sex in public bathrooms. In England, stall doors usually extend to the floor—like little cottages, how quaint!—providing maximum privacy for enterprising fellows. I'm calling it "cottaging" because the American expression "cruising" is far less specific: cruising can take place anywhere (well, maybe not so wantonly on a construction site) and doesn't even require reciprocation. The term also reminds me of the playwright Joe Orton, whose published diaries, made into the movie *Prick Up Your Ears,* contain many accounts of potty coitus, and his fellow Englishman George Michael, one of the few men outed and publicly shamed for soliciting sex in public bathrooms to make a music video satirizing the incident afterward.

It seems logical that closeted men—that included Michael before his arrest—would seek out anonymous, fleeting encounters, typically in the most transitory sorts of restrooms, at truck stops, airports, and other areas of high pedestrian traffic. But this cultural phenomenon is not limited to closeted men or even Catholic priests. So why would openly gay and bisexual men who have access to more comfortable venues like their homes, and the option of attending events such as the Black Party, an annual public sex extravaganza disguised as a dance, indulge in restroom tricks?

Men are sluts. Gay men who have embraced their slut (not technically an "inner" one) may feel they have less at stake when participating in a bit of lavatory horseplay, but the transgression and fear of being caught add an extra thrill to the experience, as Michael has admitted. Some gay men are also turned on by servicing straight guys, perhaps especially while in service stations. And no one cares about your "orientation" in a lavatory—in there, it's all business.

While I've never done it in a public bathroom (no, really!), I've been to lots of sex clubs and orgies, which I've always found cleaner and comfier. Video booths in porno shops could be a safe substitute for bathrooms, too, but if you're caught in a porno shop, you can't say you were just taking a leak. In all cases, though, the protocol is the same: a dude will grab you by the biscuits, and you can either let him continue or gently remove his hand. You may not blurt out, "Hey! Get your hands off me!" like a friend of mine once did in a back room, before he was snappily reminded of where he was. In clubs where men walk around in towels, suitors will gently tweak your nipple to gauge your interest, a greeting another friend dubbed "the Chelsea handshake."

Most homosexual men spend our formative years in the closet, and once we come out, we tend to deny that closetedness has its pleasures—and damned juicy ones, truth be told. Having a secret, perhaps double, life gives you a sense of importance, of life as drama, a sense you'll probably relish if you find yourself elected governor of New Jersey. Sex feels otherworldly, forbidden, and scary, like you've gone so deep into the closet that you've arrived in Narnia. For this reason, some openly gay men end up seeking out closets within outness: the closets of sex and/or drug addiction, fetish scenes, knitting circles—it can get crazy.

But at first it's not easy for queer goslings in the United States to find the gay world. (In a few other countries it's much easier. I'll never forget my astonishment at how many gay bars in Holland are outdoor cafes, one of which screams Gay Life in large letters across its facade; in Middle America, gay bars are still in unmarked storefronts with tinted windows.) One of the first ways you learn to find other gay Americans is to listen closely when straight people denounce homosexuals. If a relative grumbles about "faggots doing it in the park," you might think to ask, as innocently as possible, "Faggots? Really? I've never heard that. Which park? What are the cross streets?" After which you'll go there in the dead of night and find some sense of community, however narrowly focused. If a senator in your state is involved in a scandal, you might search the Internet to find his hunting grounds, even if he's not your type.

Newbies quickly learn that tapping your feet while sitting in a stall is a good way of letting other cruisers know you're on the prowl. This may be what alerted the officer who nabbed Senator Craig, and since foot tapping is such an ordinary activity, I suspect that once it becomes common knowledge, straight men will learn to keep their feet frozen stiff in the stalls. Or not.

But even these explanations for the enduring joy of cottaging seem overwrought, since what motivates a lot of men sexually is simply the prospect of easy prey with no room for intimacy. If there's one thing for which straight men envy gay men, aside from that fashion-sense stereotype, it's that we have institutions that promote no-strings sexual encounters, and that on nights when we haven't gotten lucky by last call, we can stop off at a sex club, a bar with a back room, a park, or a public bathroom to find like-minded guys, usually at no charge beyond admission. So if you're a slut and all you want is a mouth on your dick, it might not matter to you whether that hole's wearing lipstick, a goatee, or both.

Imagining that closeted gay men are the only ones involved in bathroom sex is naive, since it assumes that homosexual acts are synonymous with homosexual identity, which is silly. One hardly needs to be reminded of the many hypermasculine settings with a reputation for fostering homosexual behavior: prisons, armies, the high seas, the Village People, et cetera. (Historian B. R. Burg has argued that the seventeenth-century buccaneers of the Caribbean engaged exclusively in homosexual behavior. Take that, Johnny Depp!)

There's an age-old phenomenon known as "trade," an exchange between two men, at least one of whom is ostensibly heterosexual, in which the recipient of a blow job or the active partner in anal sex can walk away from his hanky-panky with plausible deniability. In other words, he can console himself with the belief that he is "not gay," because for some reason (misogyny, let's say) a lot of men think that whoever gets penetrated is "the woman," or more womanlike.

Which brings us back to Senator Craig. Though the *Idaho Statesman* has cataloged a series of incidents that point to homosexual pickups dating back to 1967, he's sticking to the straight story, unlike Ted Haggard, who admitted partial guilt, confessed completely and then claimed to have been "cured" after three weeks of so-called reparative therapy. So unless we can get a full, graphic report on who was planning to do what to whom in that airport bathroom stall, the senator is free to believe that he is not gay, and has never been gay. Until then, we'll all be tapping our feet.

Kids and Comstockery, Back (and Forward) in the Day

Debbie Nathan

Ah, yes, children and porn. Children *consuming* porn, I mean: a venerable American pastime. Did you know you can check out its history for free, next time you visit our nation's capital? I did and here's what I learned.

Exactly a century ago, in 1908, a middle-aged storekeeper named Pasquale Eliseo, of 119th Street and First Avenue in New York City's East Harlem, was busted on obscenity charges. His arrest happened after notorious vice czar Anthony Comstock, sneaking around town undercover, watched while Eliseo "gleefully showed his rot" to some children.

What sort of rot? Eliseo, according to Comstock, "Dealt in most sacrilegious and blasphemous books & papers. Awfull!!" (Yes, "awfull" with two *l*'s.) According to Comstock, Eliseo kept "ob."— Comstock's shorthand for "obscene"—materials in his store and "took young men into [the] basement to sell them books." Worse, he peddled ob. right on the street, where he made a habit of "exposing pictures in full view of boys and girls." These were probably "French postcards," and when Comstock happened upon Eliseo, the latter was hawking them at a penny apiece. It's not clear if he had any paying customers, but he clearly attracted some very enthusiastic young window-shoppers.

Such details come from a tall, narrow logbook that Comstock kept for decades. He used it to tabulate his obscenity arrests—in muddy, cramped handwriting, and language so fevered that it often came out misspelled and weirdly punctuated. The logbook has been microfilmed by the Library of Congress, in Washington. It's a popular item in the rare manuscripts collection there, and recently while visiting DC, I skipped the Lincoln Memorial and instead enjoyed the fruits of my taxpayer money by perusing Comstock's records.

What a glorious institution the LOC is! It houses a copy of almost every book ever published in this country (and many from other countries besides). Its librarians practically trip over themselves to help patrons. Reading rooms are well-appointed and inviting, the cafeteria food scrumptious and cheap. There's no charge to use these facilities. The LOC: a people's palace for research and knowledge. Makes you feel downright patriotic…even as you follow the creepy archival trail of federal official Comstock as he harassed citizens and worked hard to repress our culture.

A small town druggist turned moral crusader, Comstock came to power after the end of the Civil War, when he was appointed by New York State and the U.S. Post Office as *the* bigwig, antiobscenity cop. At first, he mainly went after people who advocated for and provided birth control, sex education, and other means of sexual pleasure—including toys. One such early Comstock victim is listed in his logbook as a "shrewd villain" who was "Notorious as an abortionist." There's also the "low ignorant laborer" who "advertised himself as an MD and celebrated physician for treatment of female complaints"—yet was really "An abortionist." Thanks to Comstock, this man got one year and three months at an upstate penitentiary.

Also arrested was someone named Brinckerhoff and "one Travis of Goodyear Rubber Glove Co.," who jointly "invented a substitute for a dildoe." Comstock gloated that he actually seized "the article." He added that the subsequent guilty verdict made this a "test case of great importance."

Comstock was also obsessed with protecting children from dirty materials. He wrote that he arrested a man who "used to loan the vilest Books, to young boys & girls, and sell to school children His wife to girls & he to boys & young men. He was convicted in Special Sessions, in Summer of 1868, by myself." Comstock dissed this defendant as the "Worst man in N.Y." He was sent to Blackwell's Island.

But Comstock's prosecutions were partly a losing battle.

By the 1870s, sexy pictures, texts, and tchotchkes were everywhere, in full view of the kids. In 1875, for instance, Thomas Early, twenty-three, was arrested by police in Yonkers and given three months at hard labor. His crime: distributing handbills for Kahn's Museum, on Broadway in Manhattan. Kahn's was where the public went to look at fetuses in jars, preserved cadavers, and medical specimen genitals. In Victorian America, this was how ordinary people —including women—learned about anatomy and the biology of sex. Comstock caught Early giving Kahn's flyers "indiscriminately to boys & girls." As a result, he noted in his crabbed handwriting, one child "found a book & took it to her mother to know what 'penis' meant."

Another log entry, from 1877, describes the arrest of Timothy P. Ide, nineteen, for mailing obscene pictures and books. "He advertised for 'Boys only' in various 'Boys Weekly' papers. He had three new books & was getting up another. He is a cool deliberate villain. Young as he is he surpasses many older criminals."

That same year, Mrs. Sarah E. Summers got a year of hard penal labor after Comstock's investigators found hundreds of letters and circulars in her possession, as well as articles "to prevent conception [and] procure abortion." Not only that, Comstock wrote, but Mrs. Summers had, in a popular publication, advertised the following offer: "'Girls. Secret. How to gain the love of any man for $1.00.'" For each dollar she received, Mrs. Summers sent out "her circular & a powder with written instructions to girls to mix with their own menses and administer in cold drink." Most of the letters seized were from young females, Comstock noted, including "a 16-year-old minister's daughter." Comstock must have raided this teenager's bedroom: the log notes that when discovered, she had already "sent for and administered one powder & another all prepared was found on her person."

The year 1877 also saw hanky panky with magic lanterns—contraptions that projected images in sequence to create the illusion of movement. Tremendously popular, they were forerunners to the motion picture camera. Comstock recorded that a New Yorker, Andrew Trosch, age sixty, who sold stereopticons and magic lanterns on Broome Street in Manhattan, gave a magic lantern show on the Bowery. Apparently he was projecting French postcards, or maybe just Kahn's Museum fliers. "His obscene views," Comstock wrote, "disgusted spectators. He was arrested for selling same views."

A year later, Kahn's Museum tormented again. It was displaying "wax figures of females life size, some pregnant & some otherwise & 37 cases of filthy penises. These cases were disposed of before Judge Gildersleeve."

As time passed things only got worse. In 1895, Alfred S. Thompson, of 106 E. 14th Street, was arrested for being the "manager of

6 fat women at Huber's Museum who dress in tights and ride bi-cycles. A nauseating display."

Alfred's wife, Alice, was also charged. Comstock listed her occupation as "Show Woman" and went after her because she "Sells pictures of herself in tights in a bawdy attire and posture."

Not long after, thirty-six-year-old Pauline Sheldon, of W. 98th Street, was apprehended for working at clubs such as the Black Rabbit's and the Maquet Union, on Bleeker Street. Comstock's log describes Sheldon as "A hermafadite [sic] & exhibited herself at $1 per person." She was charged with indecent exposure. Her destination was the Tombs.

During Comstock's earlier years, his busts were lauded by the establishment, including the New York Times. By the turn of the twentieth century, though, he was going stale. That's around the time he went after Ida Craddock—who today could well be described as this country's first "Dr. Ruth." A former shorthand instructor and head of "The Church of Yoga," Craddock was famous for her sex education classes and pamphlets for married couples. They extolled foreplay as vital for female pleasure, and gave detailed instructions on how to accomplish it. And to avoid unwanted pregnancy, Craddock taught men how to prevent ejaculation. All this infuriated Comstock. Craddock was busted and imprisoned so many times that the last time it happened, she couldn't take it anymore. She committed suicide by gas oven in an apartment on 23rd Street in 1902. The public was remorseful. Comstock was widely seen as a villain.

But he still had an ace in the hole: the danger of "ob." to children. Yet the kids themselves were now starting to make and distribute ob. Already in 1900, for instance, twelve-year-old Emil Grossmann, of 81 E. 11th St., had been picked up by Comstock because he "Used foul language in school room. Sent obscene letter to his teacher." Emil, Comstock wrote in his log, was "Very bawdy. A bad fellow."

Next year, Dominick Gavarse, of East Harlem, got canned for "sending obscene writing by mail to a lady teacher" at the school he attended, PS 83. "A bad boy," Comstock reiterated in his log. Dominick, twelve years old, was sent to the Tombs.

Things were getting so out of hand by then that even honor students were going wild. Louis Evenson, age thirteen, was arrested in 1902 for sending "2 ob. Letters & 1 postal card." Comstock seemed puzzled: "A well behaved boy in school," he wrote in his log. "Influenced by bad boys. Father is a Rabbi."

Perhaps if Louis and his ilk had all been unwashed, Eastern or Southern European immigrants, Comstock could have kept on going full speed. But the lad was a "German Jew," noted the logbook, and the Evensons lived right off Fifth Avenue. This junior "ob'ber" came straight out of "Our Crowd," and when New Yorkers of his stratum started crossing paths with Comstock, it couldn't have boded well for the latter's career.

Still, little Louis was a minor. Moral panic about ob's dangers to the tender aged has fueled many an inheritor to Comstock—in the bloom of the twentieth century and hard into the twenty-first. The new porny-kid "German Jews" of Fifth Avenue may be those who reside in the tony suburbs of the whole nation, or the techno-luxe cyberville of YouTube, MySpace, Facebook—or even, as in the case of Justin Berry, on their own private websites.

The Immaculate Orgasm: Who Needs Genitals?
Mary Roach

Marcalee Sipski is an expert in a field with few experts. When I tell you what the field is, you will understand why the experts are scarce. Sipski, a professor at the University of Alabama School of Medicine, is an authority on sexuality among people with spinal cord injuries and diseases. Most people, even most MDs, are uncomfortable sitting down with a paraplegic and having a talk about, say, how to have intercourse with a catheter in your penis. Sipski is fine having that talk[1], and she is fine with me coming to her lab while a subject is there.

Very little fazes Dr. Sipski. For her video *Sexuality Reborn: Sexuality Following Spinal Cord Injury*, she managed to recruit four couples to talk frankly ("...and there's the stuffing method") about how they have sex and even to demonstrate on-camera. They participated because they, like Sipski, were aware of the potentially ruinous effects of a spinal cord injury on a couple's sex life and how hard it can be to find doctors willing to address the issue in a constructive, nuts-and-bolts manner.

Sex research is a relatively recent development in Sipski's career. For years, she maintained a private practice in rehabilitation medicine. (Christopher Reeve was one of Sipski's patients, as was Ben Vereen.)[2] Over time, she grew curious about the surprisingly high percentage of patients who said they were still able to have orgasms. For decades, the medical community—being for the most part able-bodied—had assumed that people with para- and quadriplegias couldn't have them. It was a logical assumption: If a person's spinal cord is broken at a point higher than the point at which nerves from the genitals feed into the spine, then there should be no way for the nerve impulses to make their way past the injury and up to the brain. And thus, it was further assumed, no way for the person to reach orgasm.

Yet 40 to 50 percent of these men and women, according to several large surveys, do. Sipski decided to investigate. She recruited people with all different degrees and levels of spinal cord injuries for a series of studies, to see if she could find any patterns.

People with spinal cord injuries provide a unique window onto the workings of human orgasm. If you examine lots of people—some whose injuries are high on the spine, some down low, some in between—you can eventually isolate the segments of the nervous system that are crucial to orgasm. You can begin to define what exactly an orgasm is. (A recent review of the topic listed more than twenty competing definitions.) Once you have an accurate definition of what orgasm is and how it happens, then you will, hopefully, have some insight into why it sometimes doesn't. Studying people with spinal cord injuries might benefit the able-bodied as well.

It is a testament to Sipski's reputation in the disabled community that more than a hundred men and women with spinal cord injuries have traveled to her lab to be part of a study. Unless you are extremely comfortable with your sexuality, masturbating to orgasm in a lab while hooked up to a heart-rate and blood-pressure monitor is, at best, an awkward proposition. It's even more daunting when you have a spinal cord injury: among those who can reach orgasm, it takes on average about twice as long to get there. Though Sipski's subjects are alone behind a closed door, they can hear voices and sounds on the other side of the wall. They can tell that people are out there, timing them, monitoring them, waiting for them to finish.

The people out there this morning are uncommonly disruptive. This is because one of them is me, and because Sipski's colleague Paula Spath said that by climbing up onto her desk and pressing my nose up to the one-way glass, I could get a peek at the experimental setup. I have on a skirt that does not lend itself to scaling office furniture. I lost my balance and crashed into Paula's monitor, which slid across the computer it was standing on, knocking off a row of knickknacks, and causing Paula to leap back and let out the sort of high-pitched exclamation that might more appropriately be heard on the yonder side of the wall. It's a wonder anyone invites me anywhere.

A woman I'll call Gwen is under the covers inside the lab. Aside from a caddy in the corner that holds the physiological-monitoring equipment, the lab resembles a scaled-down hotel room: there is a bed with a tasteful bedspread and extraneous throw pillows, a chair, a bedside table, a framed art print, and a TV for viewing more erotic videos. Helping Gwen with her assignment is an Eroscillator 2 Plus, a vibrator endorsed by Dr. Ruth Westheimer and developed by Dr. Philippe Woog, the inventor of the first electric toothbrush.[3]

While Gwen eroscillates, Sipski explains what transpired before I arrived. All her subjects are given a physical examination to determine the extent and effects of their injury and its precise location in the spinal cord. One theory held that the people who could still have orgasms were those whose injuries were incomplete—meaning the spinal cord wasn't completely severed and that some of the nerve impulses from the genitals were squeaking through and reaching the brain. Another possibility was that the orgasmic ones were those whose breaks were below the point where the genital nerves feed into the spinal cord.

It turned out that while both these things can make a difference, neither was an ironclad deciding factor for orgasmicity. People with high spinal cord injuries could have them, and so could some with complete spinal cord injuries. Based on Sipski's data, only one thing definitively precludes orgasm: a complete injury to the sacral nerve roots at the base of the spine. Injuries here interfere with something called the sacral reflex arc, best known for its starring role in bowel and bladder function. The sacral reflex arc is part of the autonomic nervous system, the system that controls the workings of our internal organs. "Autonomic" means involuntary, beyond conscious control. The speed at which the heart beats, the peristaltic movements of the digestive system, breathing, and, to a certain extent, sexual responses, are all under autonomic control.

Sipski explains that when you damage your spinal cord, you primarily block the pathways of the somatic, not the autonomic, nervous system. Somatic nerves transmit skin sensations and willful movements of the muscles, and they travel in the spinal cord. But the nerves of the autonomic nervous system are more complicated, and not all of them run exclusively through the spinal column. The vagus nerve, for example, feeds directly from the viscera into the brain; Rutgers University researchers Barry Komisaruk and Beverly Whipple have posited that the vagus actually reaches as far down as the cervix, and that that may explain how people with spinal cord injuries feel orgasm. Either way, autonomic nerves seem to be the answer to why quadri- and paraplegics can often feel internal sensations—menstrual cramps, bowel activity, the pain of appendicitis. And orgasm.

"Think about it," Sipski is saying. "Orgasm is not a surface sensation, it's an internal sensation." Sipski routinely asks her spinal-cord-injured subjects where they stimulated themselves and where they felt the orgasm. Of nineteen women who stimulated themselves clitorally, only one reported that she'd felt the orgasm just in her clitoris. The rest ran an anatomical gamut: "bottom of stomach to toes," "head," "through vagina and legs," "all over," "from waist down," "stomach first, breast tingle, then vaginally."

It is strange to think of orgasm as a reflex, something dependably triggered, like a knee jerk. Sipski assures me that psychological factors also hold sway. Just as emotions affect heart rate and digestion, they also influence sexual response. Sipski defines orgasm as a reflex of the autonomic nervous system that can be either facilitated or inhibited by cerebral output (thoughts and feelings).

The sacral reflex definition fits nicely with something I stumbled upon in the United States Patent Office website: Patent 3,941,136, a method for "artificially inducing urination, defecation, or sexual excitation" by applying electrodes to "the sacral region on opposite sides of the spine." The patent holder intended the method to help not only people with spinal cord injuries but those with erectile dysfunction or constipation.

Best be careful, though. The nervous system can't always be trusted to keep things straight. *BJU International* tells the tale of a man who visited his doctor seeking advice about "defecation-induced orgasm." For the first ten years, the paper explains, he had enjoyed his secret neurological quirk, but he was seventy now, and it was wearing him out. Horridly, the inverse condition also exists.

Orgasm-induced defecation was noted by Alfred Kinsey to afflict "an occasional individual."

The electronics term for circuitry mix-ups is crosstalk: a signal traveling along one circuit strays from its appointed route and creates an unexpected effect along a neighboring circuit. Crosstalk explains the faint voices from someone else's conversation in the background of a telephone call. Crosstalk in the human nervous system explains not only the man who enjoyed his toilette, but also why heart attack pain is sometimes felt in the arm, and why the sensations of childbirth have been known to include orgasmic feelings or, rarely, an urge to defecate. Orgasms from nursing (or nipple foreplay) are another example of crosstalk. The same group of neurons in the brain receives sensory input both from the nipples and the genitals. They're the feel-good neurons: the ones involved in the secretion of oxytocin, the "joy hormone." (Oxytocin is involved in both orgasm and the milk-letdown reflex in nursing mothers.)

Here is something eerie about spinal reflexes: you don't need a brain. For proof of this, you need look no further than the chicken that sprints across the barnyard after its head is lopped off. Eerier still, you don't even need to be alive. The spinal reflex known as the Lazarus sign has been spooking doctors for centuries. If you trigger the right spot on the spinal cord of a freshly dead body or a beating-heart cadaver—meaning someone brain-dead but breathing via a respirator, pending the removal of organs for transplant—it will stretch out its arms and then raise them up and cross them over its chest.

How often do the dead move? A research team in Turkey, experimenting on brain-dead patients at Akdeniz University Hospital over a span of three years, was able to trigger spinal movement reflexes in 13 percent of them. (In a Korean study two years later, the figure was 19 percent.) Most of the time, the dead just jerk their fingers and toes or stretch their arms or feet, but two of the Turkish cadavers were inspired to perform the Lazarus sign.

Reflexive movements can be extremely disquieting to the medical professionals in the O.R. during organ procurement surgery—so much so that there was a push in England, around 2000, to require that anesthesia be given to beating-heart cadavers. New York lawyer-physician Stephanie Mann, who publishes frequently on the ethics of brain death and vegetative states, told me that although beating-heart cadavers may appear to be in pain, they are not. "Certainly not in the way you and I perceive pain. I think the anesthesia is administered more for the doctors' discomfort than for the cadaver's."

Mann said—because I asked her—that it might possible for a beating-heart cadaver to have an orgasm. "If the spinal cord is being oxygenated, the sacral nerves are getting oxygen, and you apply a stimulus appropriately, is it conceivable? Yes. Though they wouldn't feel it."

I tell Sipski she should do a study.

"*You* get the human subjects committee approval for that one."

"Okay!" It's Gwen's voice over the intercom. "I'm finished." She has a soft, swaying Alabama accent, "okay" pronounced UH-KAI. Paula tells Gwen to lie quietly for a few minutes and watches the monitor. She is looking for the abrupt drop-off in heart rate and blood pressure that signals that an orgasm has come and gone.

Gwen has agreed to talk with us for a few minutes before she leaves. She sits in a chair and looks at us calmly. If you did not know what she had been doing, you would not guess. Her hair is neat and her clothes are unrumpled. Only her heart rate as the experiment began (117 beats per minute) betrayed her unease.

Gwen was diagnosed with multiple sclerosis in 1999. (Sipski

began collecting orgasm and arousal data on MS patients earlier this year.) Her beauty and poise belie the seriousness of her condition. She says she is tired all the time, and her joints hurt. Her hands and feet sometimes tingle, sometimes go numb. She has trouble telling hot from cold and must have her husband check her baby's bathwater. People with MS develop lesions along their spinal cord that affect their mobility and their autonomic nervous system. Gwen's illness has affected her bowel and bladder functions as well as her sexual responsiveness: the sacral triumvirate.

"I can't feel inside," she explains. "I can't tell that I'm being penetrated I guess is what you'd say. And sometimes I can't feel stimulation on my clitoris."

Yet only six minutes had passed when she pressed the intercom button. The power of vibration to trigger orgasmic reflexes is a mystery; sometimes you don't even have to use it on the usual location. People with spinal cord injuries may develop a compensatory erogenous zone above the level of their injury. (Researchers call it "the hypersensitive area"—or, infrequently, "the oversensitive area.") Applying a vibrator to these spots can have dramatic effects, as documented by Sipski, Barry Komisaruk, and Beverly Whipple, at the Kessler Institute for Rehabilitation in Miami, where all three used to work. "My whole body feels like it's in my vagina," said the subject, a quadriplegic woman who had just had an orgasm— evinced by changes in blood pressure and heart rate—while applying a vibrator to her neck and chest. Komisaruk and Whipple's book *The Science of Orgasm* includes a description of a "knee orgasm" experienced by a young able-bodied man with a vibrator pressed to his leg. "The quadriceps muscle of the thigh increased in tension...At the reported orgasmic moment, the leg gave an extensor kick...and a forceful grunt was emitted." (In the interest of full disclosure, the young man was stoned.)

I ask Gwen how she made the decision to be part of Sipski's study. "When I first heard about it from my neurologist," she begins, "I thought, Yes, I want to do this. And then I started thinking what the situation was going to be like. And I thought, Well, I don't know if I want to or not. But me and my husband talked it over, and we thought y'all could probably help me." Gwen gets to take a vibrator home with her. The study for which she is a subject includes a treatment component comparing two stimulating tools: the FertiCare (modified with a Woog head) and the Eros. The hope is that vibration (or suction/vibration) therapy can help retrain the sacral reflex arc so that women with spinal issues can reach orgasm more easily.

Gwen retrieves her purse. She asks if we have any other questions for her.

I have one. "Did you hear a loud crash while you were in there?"

"Uh-huh. And talking."

"Sorry about that."

Sipski and I are eating at a suburban Birmingham restaurant where couples drink wine at lunch and seem to have nothing to say to each other. Or maybe they're eavesdropping. I would be.

The lunch conversation has drifted to the topic of nongenital orgasms. The ones that wake you up from dreams. The ones some epileptics[4] experience just before a seizure (and that occasionally motivate them to go off their meds). The "thought-orgasms" that ten women had in Beverly Whipple and Barry Komisaruk's Rutgers lab. The individuals Alfred Kinsey interviewed who "have been brought to orgasm by having their eyebrows stroked, or by having the hairs on some other part of their bodies gently blown, or by having pressure applied on the teeth alone." Though in the Kinsey cases, presumably other body parts had been stroked or blown just prior, and the eyebrow and tooth ministering merely, as Kinsey put it, "provided the additional impetus which is necessary to carry the individual on to orgasm."

I brought along a copy of a letter to the editors of the *British Journal of Psychiatry* entitled "Spontaneous Orgasms—Any Explanations?" The author was inquiring on behalf of a patient, a Saudi woman who had "complained bitterly of repeated uncontrolled orgasms." They happened anywhere, at any time, up to thirty times a day, "without any sort of sexual contact." Her social life had been ruined, and she had, understandably, "stopped practicing her regular religious rituals and visiting the holy shrines."

When I look up from the page, the waiter is standing with my gumbo, waiting for me to move my papers. Earlier he came over with the iced teas while Sipski was describing the bulbocavernosus reflex, which tells you whether the sacral reflex arc is intact. The test entails slipping a finger into the patient's rectum and using the other hand to either squeeze the end of the penis or touch the clitoris. If the rectum finger gets squeezed, the reflex is working. The waiters are different in Birmingham than they are in San Francisco, where I eat out. This one said simply, "Who had the unsweetened?"

Sipski's explanation for nongenital orgasms is this: You are triggering the same reflex, just doing it via different pathways. "There's no reason why the impulses couldn't travel down from the brain, rather than up from the genitals." The input would be neurophysiological in the case of epilepsy patients and the Saudi woman, psychological in the case of the Kinsey folks.

Sexual arousal, not just orgasm, reflects this bidirectional split. Here again, spinal cord injuries have helped researchers tease apart the two systems: there is "reflex arousal" and there is "psychological arousal." If you show erotic films to someone with a complete injury high up on the spinal cord, the person may say they find the images arousing, but that psychogenic input will be blocked from traveling down the spine, and thus no lubrication (or erection) will ensue. These people can, however, get erections or lubrication from physical, or "reflex," stimulation of their genitals.

Very low spinal cord injuries create the opposite dichotomy: the person can only become lubricated from seeing (or reading or listening to) something erotic. Physical "reflex" arousal is blocked by the injury. Able-bodied men and women respond to both kinds of input. Their orgasms can be triggered by a single type of input, or a combination. Barry Komisaruk calls the latter "blended orgasms." This might explain why the single-malt orgasms—vaginal, clitoral, nongenital—all feel somewhat different.

There's one more varietal orgasm I want to ask Sipski about: the kind some kids have climbing the ropes in gym class. Sipski wasn't one of those kids. "I have never heard of this." We both look at each other like we're nuts. I explain that it isn't from contact with the rope, but more from the lifting of your body. Sipski replies that this makes sense, as orgasms from squeezing the pelvic and/or buttock muscles are not unheard of. Kinsey mentions having interviewed some men and "not a few" women who use this technique to arouse themselves and who "may occasionally reach orgasm without the genitalia being touched."

Sipski suspects that this might be how the hands-free orgasm women in the Rutgers lab were managing it. She doesn't know that three weeks before I had lunch with her, I went out for sushi with one of those women. Kim Airs, whose contact information I got from Barry Komisaruk, happened to be in my city visiting friends and agreed to meet to talk about her unique skill set. Airs is a tall, ebullient woman in her forties whose past employers include porn production companies, an escort service, and Harvard University, where she worked with then-president Lawrence Summers. Airs learned the "hands-free" technique in 1995, in a breath-and-energy orgasm workshop taught by sex-worker-turned-sex-educator Annie Sprinkle[5] It took her two years to master the craft. Now she can do it easily and upon request, which she does in workshops and talks and, occasionally, on sidewalk benches outside sushi bars.

It was nothing like the *When Harry Met Sally* scene. The people walking past had no idea. She closed her eyes and took some long, slow breaths and after maybe a minute of this, her face flushed pink and she shuddered. If you weren't watching closely, you'd think she was a runner who'd stopped on a bench to catch her wind.

Like the orgasms of Sipski's subjects, those of Airs and Komisaruk's other volunteers were verified by monitoring heart rate and blood pressure. Definitively verifying someone's claim to an orgasm is more difficult than Masters and Johnson would have you believe. The duo described telltale muscle contractions, but Sipski found that not all women have these.[6] The steep rise and abrupt postorgasm drop-off in heart rate and systolic blood pressure are the closest there is to a reliable physiological marker. Airs made the grade.

Sipski is right that at least some of the thought orgasms were helped along by internal muscle flexing. At the end of their paper, Whipple and Komisaruk state that some of the women were making "vigorous muscular movements," and concede that the others may have been doing so more subtly. A how-to web article under Annie Sprinkle's byline includes directions to squeeze the pelvic floor muscles in order to "stimulate the clitoris and G spot." (Arnold Kegel years ago found that diligent Kegelers tend to have an easier time of orgasm.)

Airs herself, however, described a process involving chakras and waves of energy, but no interior calisthenics. She appeared to be taking herself into an altered state, which makes sense, because that seems to be where people go during an orgasm. Scans show that the brain's higher faculties quiet down, and more primitive structures light up. As in most altered states, people tend to lose their grip on time. In 1985, sex physiologist Roy Levin brought twenty-eight women into his lab and timed their orgasms. After they'd finished, he asked them to estimate how long the orgasm had lasted. With only three exceptions, the estimates were well under the real duration—by an average of thirteen seconds. Orgasm appears to be a state not unlike that of the alien abductees one always hears about, coming to with messy hair and a chunk of time unaccounted for.

What is life like for someone who can discreetly trigger an orgasm with a few moments of mental effort? Airs insists she rarely undertakes it in public. "Sometimes on long plane flights," she said. The last time was while riding the Disneyland tram.

Nor is it, in the privacy of her home, a nightly occurrence. "Usually when I get home I'm too tired."

NOTES:

1. "The catheter can be folded back over the penis and both the penis and catheter covered with a condom."

2. Vereen came in for rehabilitation after he was struck by a car (though not paralyzed) while walking on the Pacific Coast Highway some years back. Sipski recruited Vereen to do the introduction on *Sexuality Reborn*, which he undertook with admirable dignity and no dancing.

3. For years, Dr. Woog had been aware that women were using his inventions as a vibrator. Every now and then, returned toothbrushes that passed through quality control "clearly seemed to have been used in that way," said his son Lionel Woog, who oversees marketing for the vibrator company Advance Response. At a certain point, a light bulb went on in the elder Woog's head, and he set to work on a vibrator. "It's the same idea," said Lionel. "You want to stimulate the tissue without damaging it." Lionel told me the story of the Eskimos, and how their gums deteriorated when they moved to settlements and began eating processed foods instead of raw animal parts. Vigorous chewing, he explained, stimulates bone growth and keeps gums healthy. Woog's Broxodent electric toothbrush used to be given to marines on nuclear submarines. "They ate a lot of canned foods," said Woog, and the toothbrush helped keep their gums in shape. It was a popular item with the men, maybe even for that reason. As Lionel Woog says, "You have to masticate."

4. The most interesting being the woman in Taiwan who, once or twice a week, would have an

orgasm (followed by a mild nonconvulsive seizure) when she brushed her teeth. The smell of toothpaste alone wouldn't trigger it, nor was it limited to any specific brand. It didn't happen when she poked at her gums with a chopstick or when she moved her empty fist back and forth in a tooth-brushing motion. Curious neurologists at Chang Gung Memorial Hospital gave her a toothbrush and toothpaste and hooked her up to an EEG. Sure enough, after thirty-eight seconds of the "highly specific somatosensory stimulus" we call toothbrushing, it happened. The woman, whose case report appears in a 2003 issue of *Seizure*, was neither delighted nor amused by the situation. She believed she was possessed by demons, and soon switched to mouthwash for her oral hygiene.

5. Highly decorated in both pursuits, Sprinkle holds a PhD in human sexuality as well as a spot on the Adult Star Path of Fame in Edison, New Jersey. The Path of Fame was the brainchild of Mike Drake, manager of the Edison porn emporium Playtime. Drake also oversaw the contents of Playtime's Adult Time Capsule, which include an autographed CyberSkin replica of Sprinkle's vagina. Other items bound to confuse the earthlings of 2069 include nipple clamps, a Decadent Indulgence Vibrator with rotating pleasure beads and "clitoral hummingbird vibrator," and a set of "starter anal beads."

6. She figured this out by borrowing a perinometer, a contraction-measuring device first built by Arnold Kegel to document the vaginal strength gains of Kegeling women. To this same end, Kegel made Before and After plaster casts of women's vaginas, to show that their Kegeling regime had rendered them firmer and less "gaping," to use the terminology of Kegel's colleague Marilyn Fithian. "You had to get the plaster out before it got too hard," Fithian told me in an interview years ago. Otherwise, it would get stuck, and no amount of pelvic floor muscle strength was going to help you. "You had to break it inside the vagina," said Fithian, who was in her seventies then and still Kegeling.

About the Authors

BRIAN ALEXANDER is the author of several books including *America Unzipped: The Search for Sex and Satisfaction*, currently out in paperback. He has also written for many magazines and newspapers including the *New York Times*, the *Los Angeles Times, Wired, Esquire, Glamour, Science*, and many more. He writes the "Sexploration" column for MSNBC.com, and has made many television and radio appearances.

VIOLET BLUE is the *San Francisco Chronicle*'s sex columnist, a Forbes Web Celebrity, and one of *Wired*'s Faces of Innovation 2008. She is the best-selling, award-winning author and editor of more than two dozen books on sexual health and erotica, with translations worldwide. Blue writes about sexuality for publications such as *Forbes* and *O: The Oprah Magazine,* and lectures to cyberlaw classes at UC Berkeley, tech conferences (ETech), sex crisis counselors at community teaching institutions, and Google Inc. Her website is tinynibbles. com, her tech site is techyum.com, and her audio and ebooks are self-published with multiple authors at digitapub.com. Webnation labeled Blue "the leading sex educator for the Internet generation."

SUSANNAH BRESLIN is working on a novel based on her experiences in Porn Valley. She has written for *Details, Harper's Bazaar, Newsweek,* Salon, Radar Online, and many other publications. Her blog, Reverse Cowgirl (reversecowgirlblog.blogspot.com), was named one of Time.com's Top 25 Blogs in 2008.

TRACY CLARK-FLORY is a writer and assistant editor for the online magazine Salon. Her musings on politics and pop culture can be found on Salon's lady blog, Broadsheet. For more, visit her website, www.tracyclark-flory.com.

KELLY DAVIS is the associate editor for *San Diego City Beat,* the alternative newsweekly she helped cofound in 2002. Her reporting focuses on subjects such as homelessness, drug addiction, and criminal-justice policies.

STACEY D'ERASMO is the author of the novels *Tea* (2000), *A Seahorse Year* (2004), and the forthcoming *The Sky Below* (2009). She is an assistant professor of writing at Columbia University.

TRACIE EGAN is an editor at the women's website Jezebel.com. She lives in Brooklyn with her dog Edie.

KEEGAN HAMILTON is a native of Seattle, Washington. He is a graduate of the University of Washington School of Communications, class of 2007. He was a recipient of the *Village Voice* Media

Editorial Fellowship and has been a staff writer at the *Riverfront Times* since December 2007. His work has also appeared in the *Seattle Weekly*, the *Nashville Scene* and the *West Seattle Herald*.

JAMES HANNAHAM is a staff writer in the culture department at Salon.com. His first novel, *God Says No*, published by McSweeney's Books in 2009, contains more than one bathroom sex scene.

LYNN HARRIS (www.lynnharris.net) is an award-winning journalist and author. Her most recent novel is the satirical mystery *Death By Chick Lit*. She contributes frequently to *Glamour*, the *New York Times*, Salon.com, Nerve.com, Nextbook.org, and many others, and she is cofounder of the venerable website BreakupGirl.net.

DAGMAR HERZOG is professor of history at the Graduate Center of the City University of New York. She is the author of, most recently, *Sex in Crisis: The New Sexual Revolution and the Future of American Politics*, as well as two pioneering books, *Intimacy and Exclusion* and *Sex After Fascism*, as well as numerous scholarly articles on the history of sexuality.

TOM JOHANSMEYER is a New York-based freelance writer who covers the adult entertainment industry. In addition to writing AVN Online's "Money Matters" column, Tom has written several investigative pieces, from debunking the claim that tax stimulus checks were being spent on porn to the confiscation of adult novelty items from civilian contractors serving in Iraq. His work has appeared in *Boston* magazine, *Penthouse*, *Trader Monthly*, and *Cigar Report*, among others.

ALAN R. LEVY is a senior associate in the New York City office of

Sedgwick, Detert, Moran, & Arnold, LLP and is a member of the firm's Media, Entertainment, and Sports Law Practice Group. He can be reached at ALevy1@aol.com.

DAVID LEVY is an· internationally recognized expert on artificial intelligence. He is president of the International Computer Games Association and in 1997 led the team that won the Loebner Prize— the world championship for conversational computer software. In 2006, he became the first person ever to present papers on intimate relationships with robotic partners at an international conference. He is the author of *Love and Sex with Robots: The Evolution of Human-Robot Relationships* and *Robots Unlimited*. Levy lives in London with his wife, Christine, and their cat.

KRISTINA LLOYD is the author of three erotic novels, *Darker Than Love, Asking for Trouble,* and *Split,* all published by Black Lace. Her short stories have appeared in numerous anthologies and magazines both in the United Kingdom and the United States, and her novels have been translated into German, Dutch, and Japanese. She has a master's distinction in Twentieth Century Literature, and has been described as "a fresh literary talent" who "writes sex with a formidable force." She lives in Brighton on the south coast of England. For more, visit http://kristinalloyd.wordpress.com.

MISTRESS MORGANA MAYE is an experienced San Francisco-based BDSM professional and sex educator. Her workshops on BDSM have delighted thousands of kink-curious people of all persuasions, and she is the cowriter and host of the instructional video *Whipsmart: A Good Vibrations Guide to SM for Beginning Couples.* Her writing has appeared in *Best American Erotica 2005* and *Politically Inspired*. Mistress Morgana believes that the current Bush administration is neither safe, sane, nor consensual and could learn a great deal from the ethics of BDSM play.

DAPHNE MERKIN is a cultural critic who has made a name for herself with her often-unnerving candor and elegantly High/Low reflections on issues of family, religion, psychotherapy and sex. She was a staff writer for the *New Yorker* for five years, where she wrote a movie column, book reviews and articles about subjects as varying as Marilyn Monroe, Freud, and Bridget Jones. She is currently a contributing writer for the *New York Times Magazine,* where she writes profiles and personal essays as well as on topics like the search for the perfect perfume and her obsession with handbags for the *Times* "T" sections; her work appears regularly in Slate and *Elle* and in a variety of other publications, including *Vogue, Travel &Leisure,* and *Allure.* Ms. Merkin is the author of two books: an autobiographical novel, *Enchantment,* which won the Edward Lewis Wallant award in 1986 for the best new work of fiction based on a Jewish theme, and *Dreaming of Hitler,* a collection of essays. She lives in New York City with her daughter.

New York City-based DEBBIE NATHAN writes a lot about anxieties over boundaries—national, racial, ethnic, and gender-based— and about how these fears often get displaced into sex panics. She's especially interested in child sex abuse hysterias and was one of the first journalists to critically cover the 1980s "satanic daycare center" panic. She is author of *Women and Other Aliens: Essays from the U.S.- Mexico Border* and co-author of *Satan's Silence: Ritual Abuse and the Making of a Modern American Witch Hunt.* She's currently working on a book about the making of the 1970s bestseller *Sybil.* Her blog is www.debbienathan.com.

MARY ROACH is the author of the *New York Times* bestsellers *Stiff: The Curious Lives of Human Cadavers, Spook: Science Tackles the Afterlife,* and *Bonk: The Curious Coupling of Science and Sex. Stiff* has been translated into 16 languages, and *Spook* was a New York Times Notable Book of 2005. Mary has written for *Outside, National Geographic, Wired, New Scientist,* the *New York Times Magazine,* and NPR's "All Things Considered." She has been a contributing editor at the science magazine *Discover,* a frequent contributor to the *New York Times Book Review,* a National Magazine Award finalist, and a winner of the American Engineering Societies' Engineering Journalism Award, in a category for which, let's be honest, she was the sole entrant. Read more at www.maryroach.net.

AMANDA ROBB is a contributing writer at *O: The Oprah Magazine,* currently at work on a book about the abstinence movement. Her journalism has also appeared in a the *New York Times, Newsweek, George, Marie Claire,* and *More* magazines. Robb won a 2008 Sexie Award for an op-ed that appeared in the *New York Times* about federal funding for abstinence-only education and a 2003 Writers Guild Award for scriptwriting on the soap opera "All My Children." Today she lives with her husband and daughter in New York City.

"JOSEPHINE THOMAS" is the pseudonym of a freelance writer whose work has appeared in *Health, Self, Redbook, Marie Claire, Parents,* and *Parenting.* She lives with her husband and two children.

DON VAUGHAN is a freelance writer based in Raleigh, North Carolina. His work appears regularly in an eclectic array of publications, including *Military Officer Magazine, Nursing Spectrum, Heal Magazine, Penthouse Forum,* and *Mad* Magazine. In addition,

Vaughan has written, cowritten, ghosted, or contributed to twenty-five books on topics ranging from the Civil War to attention deficit hyperactivity disorder. He is also the founder of Triangle Area Freelancers (www.triangleareafreelancers.org), the largest organization in North Carolina devoted to freelance writing.

Milwaukee native DAN VEBBER served His Country as one of the first editors of the *Onion* before writing for *Space Ghost Coast to Coast, Daria, Futurama, American Dad,* and other such programs catering to the valuable stoned-kids-who-light-their-farts demographic. He currently resides in Development Hell, where his projects include a stapled, Xeroxed packet of his cartoons rejected by the *New Yorker,* due to be sent to his mother sometime in '08.

About the Editor

RACHEL KRAMER BUSSEL (www.rachelkramerbussel.com) is an author, editor, blogger, and reading series host. She has edited or coedited more than twenty books of erotica, including *Tasting Him; Tasting Her; Spanked: Red-Cheeked Erotica; Naughty Spanking Stories 1* and *2; Yes, Sir; Yes, Ma'am; He's on Top; She's on Top; Caught Looking; Hide and Seek; Crossdressing; Rubber Sex; Sex and Candy; Ultimate Undies; Glamour Girls; Bedding Down;* and *Best Sex Writing 2008.* Her work has been published in more than one hundred anthologies, including *Best American Erotica 2004* and *2006,* Zane's *Chocolate Flava 2* and *Purple Panties, Everything You Know About Sex is Wrong, Single State of the Union,* and *Desire: Women Write About Wanting.* She serves as senior editor at *Penthouse Variations,* and wrote the popular "Lusty Lady" column for the *Village Voice.*

Rachel has written for *AVN, Bust,* Cleansheets.com, *Cosmopolitan, Curve,* Fresh Yarn, The Frisky, Gothamist, Huffington Post,

Mediabistro, *Newsday, New York Post, Penthouse, Playgirl, Radar, San Francisco Chronicle, Tango, Time Out New York,* and *Zink,* among others. She has been quoted in the *New York Times, USA Today, Maxim UK, Glamour UK, GQ Italy, National Post* (Canada), *Wysokie Obcasy (Poland), Seattle Weekly,* and other publications, and has appeared on "The Martha Stewart Show," "The Berman and Berman Show," NY1, and Showtime's "Family Business." She has hosted In The Flesh Erotic Reading Series since October 2005, about which the *New York Times*'s UrbanEye newsletter said she "welcomes eroticism of all stripes, spots, and textures." She blogs at lustylady. blogspot.com and cupcakestakethecake.blogspot.com.